The

... can be used by a GM to ... quickly:

Lay the book flat, back c...

Drop a handful of d4s o...

Look at where the dice landed. ... eft of a die shows the "to hit" number "rolled".

Looking down from there will show the damage if it's a weapon doing d8 damage, looking up will show damage if it's a weapon doing d6, and the die itself will show the damage if it's a d4 weapon.

Optionally, looking to the right will show the location of each hit, with higher numbers indicating more vital areas – or the die can be re-rolled.

he die roll and die position in the picture below...

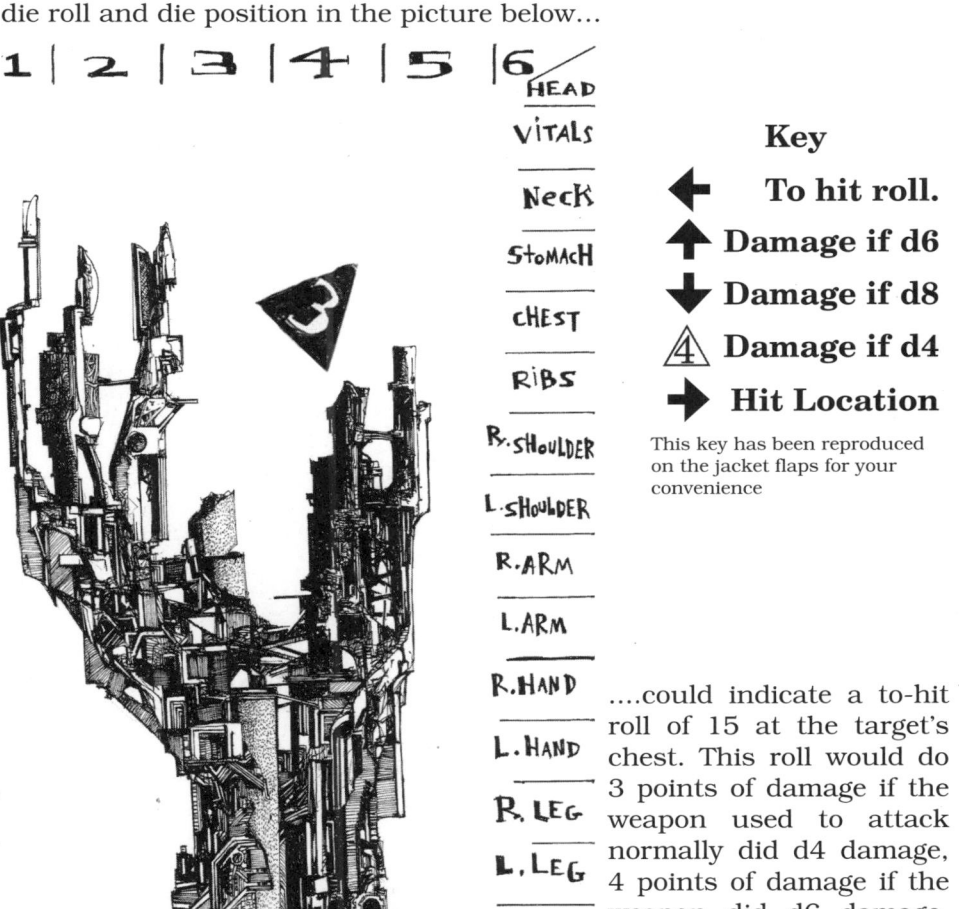

Key

← To hit roll.
↑ Damage if d6
↓ Damage if d8
△ Damage if d4
→ Hit Location

This key has been reproduced on the jacket flaps for your convenience

....could indicate a to-hit roll of 15 at the target's chest. This roll would do 3 points of damage if the weapon used to attack normally did d4 damage, 4 points of damage if the weapon did d6 damage, and 5 points of damage if the weapon did d8.

> "All things weird are normal in this whore of cities"
> -Lemmy Caution, *Alphaville*

Inner Vornheim Map..................Inside Jacket	Floorplan Shortcut 38
Game Element Generator ....Front Cover	The Law 39
Generator Instructions....Inside Front Cover	Contacts..39
Introduction..2	Optional Rules for Chases...................40
Around Vornheim 3	Item Cost Shortcut..............................40
Palace Massive......................................4	Optional Rules for Libraries 41
Eminent Cathedral 5	Notes on Open-Ended City Adventures 42
In Vornheim 6	Further Reading..................................42
The Basics......................................6	God's Chess 43
Oddities of the City 7	Table Explanations 44
Superstitions of Vornheim 9	Aristocrats Table 46
House of the Medusa Introduction 11	Books Table...48
House of the Medusa Map 12	City NPCs Table...................................50
House of the Medusa Map Kay 13	City Shopkeepers Table.......................52
House of the Medusa Stats and Details.......15	Contacts Table 52
Immortal Zoo of Ping Feng Introduction ...16	Directions Table 53
Immortal Zoo of Ping Feng Details...............17	Connections Between NPCs Diagram 53
Immortal Zoo of Ping Feng Map 18	Encounters Table 54
Immortal Zoo of Ping Feng Map Key...........19	Fortunes Table 56
Immortal Zoo of Ping Feng Details..............20	"I Search the Body" Table 58
Library of Zorlac Introduction 24	Legal Situations Table.........................59
Library of Zorlac Map.....................................26	Magic Effects Table..............................60
Library of Zorlac Map Key.............................27	Taverns and Games Table 62
Library of Zorlac Stats and Details.............28	Late Edition Conversions 64
Player Commentaries 32	Buildings Table.................Inside Back Cover
Typical Tower of Vornheim...........................34	Multiple Hit Generator................ Back Cover
Urbancrawl Rules...35	

Art & Writing:
Zak S.

Graphic Design:
James Edward Raggi IV, Zak S. and Jeremy Jagosz

Type 4 Translations:
Darren Eskandari

Map Coloring Assist:
Mandy Morbid

Proofreading:
Maria Kyytinen

Original Vorhnheim Campaign Players:
Adrienne Anderson, Shawn Cheng, Connie, Darren Eskandari, Sasha Grey, Frankie, Justine Joli, Gia Jordan, Kimberly Kane, Sean McCarthy, John Mejias, Mandy Morbid & her siblings, Chris Patch, Roger Peffley, Satine Phoenix, Caroline Pierce, Steve Prue, Bobbi Starr, Steve, Stoya, Craig Taylor, Vivka, Matt Wiegle

Other Playtesters:
Tavis Allison, Joe Burns, David Cameron, Pablo Clark, Sam Deere, Duke Dukellis, Ken Fernandez, Carl Foner, Nikolai Fullman, Eric Gall, Ian Gardocki, Tim Jenkins, James King, Thaddeus King, Ara Kooser, Terran Lane, Steve Lightsey, Chris Lowrance, Michael Marshall, Patrick Mastrobuono, Jed McClure, Mike Monaco, Tom Monaco, Chris Newman, Håkon Nordheim, DJ Papcin, James Edward Raggi IV, Susan Rati-Lane, Aron Riktor, Adrian Romero, James Schmitz, Martin Skullerud, George Strayton, Richard Sullivan, John Ughrin, Sven Roald Undheim, Lon Varnadore, Craig Wilson

Special thanks to whoever designed the cover of Black Sabbath *Vol 4*

Dedicated to Simon Tilbrook and Alan Hunter- we owe you so much.

Introduction

Vast is Vornheim, The Grey Maze, its towered alleys sprawling through the winds of the polar plain like a long-spined insect frozen in time... but I'm not here to bore you with that. This book is not about Vornheim, it's about *running* Vornheim – or any other city – in a fantastic Medieval setting. And about running it with a minimum of hassle, so you and your players can get to the good stuff. Too often, I find, city supplements start by inspiring you and finish by exhausting you – every time the characters need a hatpin or a halberd, you have to go scurrying back to the map or the index to find out where the appropriate merchant's set up shop.

So while I hope you'll walk away from this book remembering that the Palace Massive and Eminent Cathedral erupt from the apex of a wracked and rigid skyline like a pair of great claws seeking the moon, what I hope even more is that you'll walk away with some useful ideas about what to do with a Palace Massive or Eminent Cathedral, or a Randomly Generated Cheese Shop. To this end, this supplement is less about floorplans, major NPCs, and conspiracies that threaten to annihilate all the civilized nations of the earth and more about ways to quickly and easily generate floorplans, major NPCs, and conspiracies that threaten to annihilate all the civilized nations of the earth in the middle of a session while the players are breathing down your neck waiting for you to tell them what's going on. That's why we called it a 'Kit' – you can use it to build your own city, even in the middle of a game. Give somebody a floorplan and they'll GM for a day – show them how to make 30 floorplans in 30 seconds and they'll GM forever.

That said, anyone hoping they bought a book containing The Real Vornheim That The D&D With Pornstars Girls Play In has got it. These are our rules and tables and monsters and places. I wouldn't want to spend all this time writing a book I couldn't use.

Feel free to fill in any gaps as you see fit. *Any detail of the rules or setting left unexplained has been left that way because it's not important to the character of the setting, and the GM should interpret it however s/he feels will distribute maximum fun.* Where's the prison? If I wrote it down, then you'd have to look it up, and Vornheim is still Vornheim no matter where you put the prison, so I didn't (I did make a map with some places you could put it, though). Is this NPC more than just a cackling fiend? It's more fun to decide than to remember. How much damage does slicing the dog out of a victim of a *Vile Hound* spell do? It's up to you. Knock yourself out.

This book does contain some material that's been published elsewhere – often for free. Due to the scope of this project, it's sort of unavoidable – without things like the "Urbancrawl Rules", this could hardly be called a "complete city kit". *I* wanted this volume to include everything *I* need to run a city adventure and that, unfortunately, includes things some of you may have seen before. If so, write to me and ask for any tables, rules, or setting details you wish were included instead of the old material and I'll think something up and send it to you if I get a minute.

Zak S
http://dndwithpornstars.blogspot.com

I've never much liked city adventures. I know cities of any notable size are unique (just travel a bit and you'll see this is true) but all the cities in my games end up looking more or less the same. Why? Making cities unique is a lot of work when you're not really sure if the PCs are going to stick around or if they're just interested in staying the night and buying rations before moving on. So I was excited when I got this book and saw that Vornheim completely solves that problem. All the hustle and bustle of cities in general is handled by the Urbancrawl Rules, and the tables are a template you can use to customize any city and make it as unique as it should be. This means more city adventures in my campaigns because now I know how to make them *good*.

Two notes for those using Vornheim with Weird Fantasy Role-Playing: Vornheim assumes the gold standard, and the armor classes given assume unarmored characters are AC 10.

James Edward Raggi IV, Publisher

While GMs are free to put the city anyplace they want on the campaign map (or anyplace cold at least), cities are, to some degree, defined by their neighbors. All the following places can be potential allies, enemies, rivals, or trading partners of Vornheim, and send visitors there.

A. **A Forest** – How the twisted and eternally leafless trees of the north survive is unclear. Some claim they are a phlegmatic species of undead.

B. **Nornrik** emerges as the trees thin. Not all the white elves are barbaric and pitiless – some are civilized and pitiless. This is their city. They are ruled by two blue-skinned sisters, frost giant queens.

C. Halfway to Nornrik, in the center of the forest, lies Osc Leth, which Lord Eisengeth rules from a crooked tower, advised by six monstrous wives: a maggot naga, twin harpies, a cannibalistic seamaid, a fat succubus, and a hollow bride.

D. **Gaxen Kane**. Little is known about the goblin city. It is said the inhabitants speak backwards and walk on the ceiling.

E. On a plain near the town of Olgrave two great armies stand enmeshed and unmoving in a white web, held unchanging in the midst of mutual slaughter. The forces of the mad wizard Gorth and a hybrid band of desperate allies scraped together to oppose him have faced each other thus for 4,000 years. One day the white strands will fray, the battle will continue, and the ancient forces of Gorth the Unfathomable will once more seek to maraud, to devastate, and to overthrow.

F. **Bellet Osc** – Roaming the streets at night in a motley parade, wearing animal masks, waving torches, and hitting each other with fish parts mounted on sticks, the citizens of Bellet Osc are all mad. The ancient center of the city, however, lurks quietly behind walls and clear water. It is a forbidden place, home to the Hex King, a lich. 7 black swans swim the moat. Allegedly founded long ago as a leprosarium for Vornheim's afflicted.

G. **The Island of Nephilidia**. Amphibious vampires rule its tarnished palaces and rotting halls – forever knee-deep in black and stagnant water, with strange algaes stretched like cobwebs from the surface to the once-ornate walls and crumbling statuary – endlessly elaborating cruel and languid intrigues, attended by salamander men and fish without eyes.

The entire planet is a hive of stone tunnels carved by long-dead civilizations. Familiar landscape features – trees, grass, seas and oceans – form but a thin layer on top of this gigadungeon, and the ruins of nameless cities punch through the crust in every direction.

Palace Massive

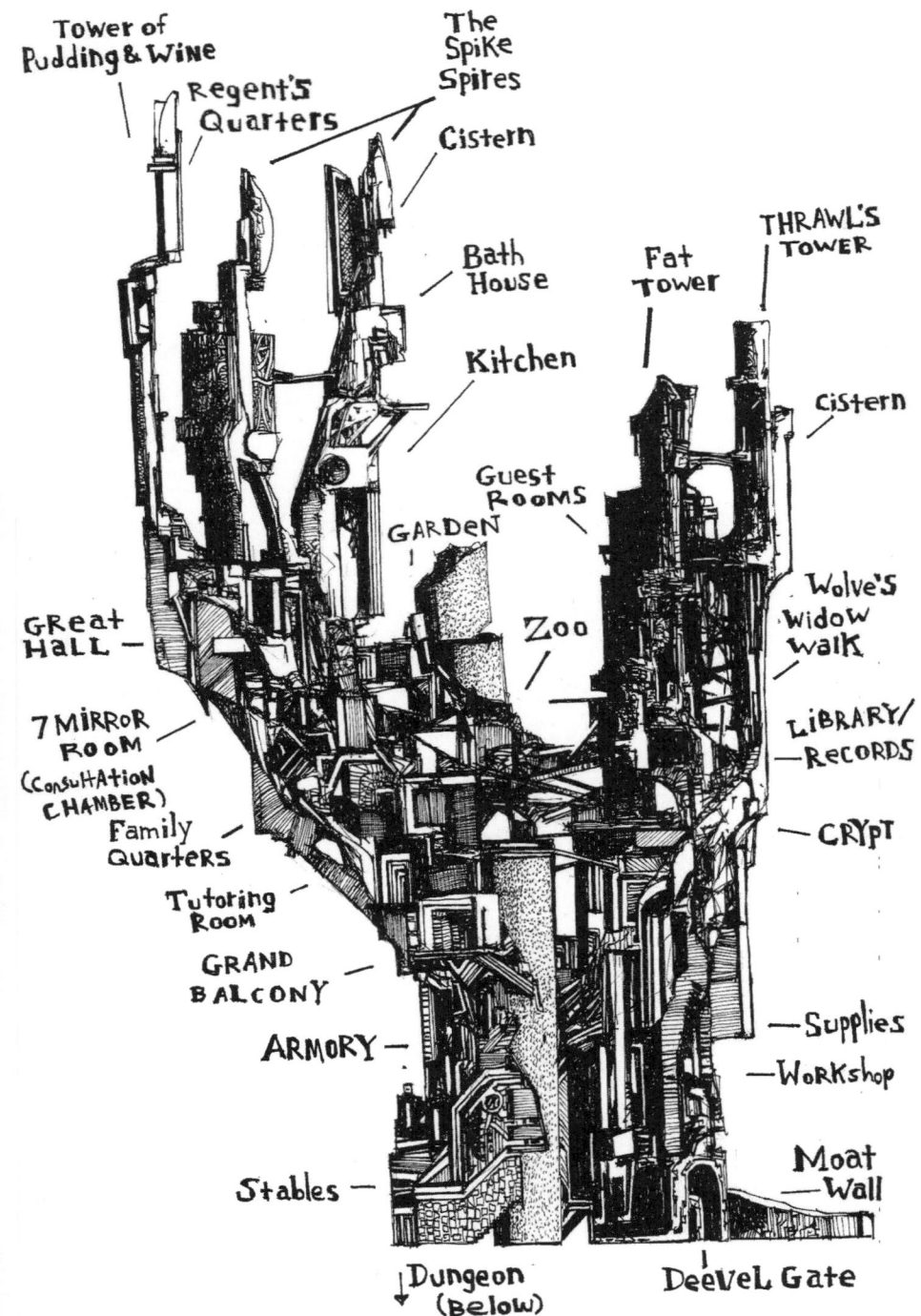

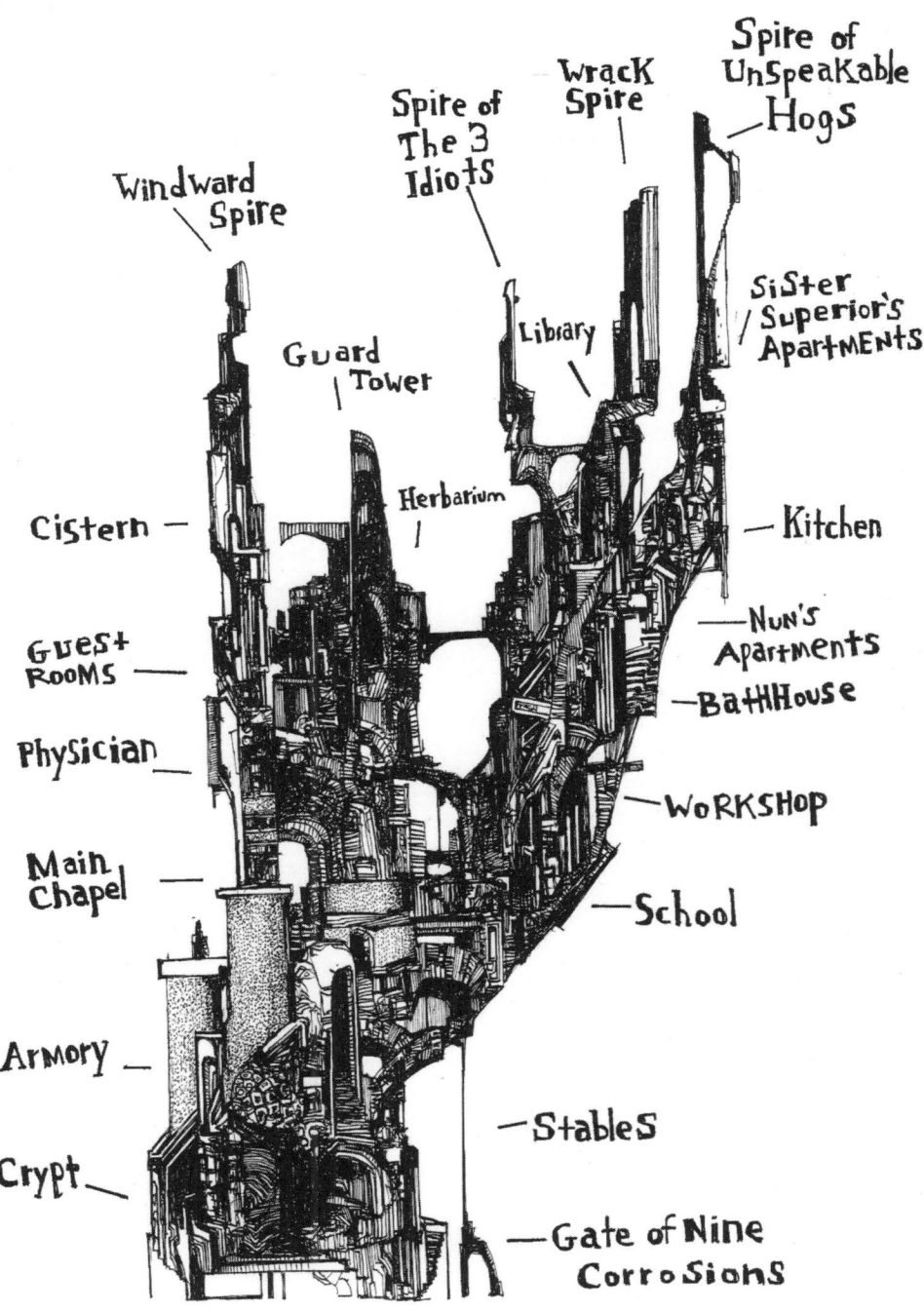

Eminent Cathedral

Some People, Places, Things and Ideas in Vornheim

Note it doesn't say "*Important* People, Places Things and Ideas" because few of them are indispensable to the character of the city. Like most game settings, this one was built piece-by-piece, in play, and it was Vornheim all along...

NPCs and monsters in this section have generally not been given stats because there's no particular reason they couldn't be built to fit adventures for any level.

The Basics

Most of the residents of Vornheim are human, though elves are common – particularly the long-haired, sharp-fanged white elves of the north – and dwarves are not unknown. The city is landlocked, and shipping comes in from the River of Unfathomable Despair through miles of underground tunnels. The typical Vornheim vista is equal parts snow and stone. The streets are narrow, and the basic unit of building is the stone tower.

Vornheim is protected by two **walls**: one circling Inner Vornheim, and another girdling the outskirts of the city. Remains of ancient walls are scattered throughout the city.

Practically speaking, **magic** is uncommon, and even the simplest cantrip will provoke awe in onlookers. Magic is never used as a "technology". However, curious adventurers who plunge into the city will find that there is in fact a great deal of the supernatural below the surface.

There are thousands of **guilds and organizations** in Vornheim, but few are organized or powerful enough to wield influence throughout the entire city. Assume there are at least 2d4 trade (price-fixing) guilds for every profession. It's the author's opinion that the clear presentation of various societies, thieves' guilds, and cults in city supplements generally makes a city feel small and comprehensible, and this is not what we're going for here. Associations and small conspiracies metastasize and meld throughout Vornheim like shadows in torchlight, making it difficult, in the interlinked enormity, to clearly divide one from the next.

A number of **bridges** have been built to facilitate movement between the city's towers. Many are fully or partially covered to protect travelers from the wind. Many also contain stone pipes allowing them to function as aqueducts – melting snow is caught in the collars around the towers' pointed domes and channelled to provide water to the lower echelons of the city.

Though the **armament laws** are unevenly enforced from neighborhood to neighborhood, openly carrying most weapons is illegal for anyone other than city guards, militiamen, etc. Nobles may carry daggers and rapiers.

There are a number of **sumptuary laws** preventing citizens of low station from wearing ostentatious fashions such as pointed shoes and flamboyant hats.

The Palace Massive once was home to wise Lord Thrawl, but his current whereabouts are mysterious. A series of regents and administrators vie for power in his absence, while all good people pray for his return. The palace's consultation chamber contains 7 magic mirrors, which allow leaders to consult 7 sides of themselves. A spore-filled murk coats the moat.

The Church of Vorn – Grim Gaunt God of Iron, Rust and Rain – is the most powerful in Vornheim. Its seat is the Eminent Cathedral.

The Church of Tittivilla – the Horned Queen, Goddess of All Flesh – once built its temples inside the living bodies of Sacred Beasts (colossal goat-like creatures) – but, so far as anyone knows, none remain. The church still operates out of ordinary buildings all over the continent.

Vosculous Eeeben is the current Duke Regent of Vornheim. Like most who have donned the Three Beaked Mask of the Regent, he is a vain compromiser, given to fits of solitary drinking. His only joy is gambling in the grub-breeding pits. Like most nobles of his line, his mother began exposing him to small doses of poison as a child so that, by the age of 13, he'd built up an immunity to most common toxins.

Oddities of the City

The strangest and most common form of **theatre** in Vornheim is descended from the brutal operas of the Reptile Men, and requires actors to both improvise within given roles and engage in ritual combat at crucial moments – the results of these battles decide the outcome of the plot. Few of these entertainments end the same way twice. Some plays are said to tell the future, some decide the fate of criminals (see Legal Situations pg 59), some enact rituals meant to aid the citizens in times of need.

The upper classes of Vornheim are fond of cultivating great **gardens** in black, blue, magenta and aqua, thick with exotic (and sometimes dangerous) species crossbred to resist the cold. Such gardeners are often fickle – and will abandon unpromising projects, allowing them to grow wild and strange, down alleyways and between towers like narrow jungles while the gardeners move on to grow new plants in new neighborhoods.

Another common aristocratic diversion is the care and breeding of **slow pets**. Originally conceived as a way for the owner to display his or her indolence (and therefore status), a slow pet can be any small animal that takes an inordinately long time to move and therefore presents the owner who walks it as one possessing an enviable surfeit of disposible time. Among the most popular are: black lobsters, blue lobsters, and alchemically-enhanced turtles with bizarre, shaped shells. Particularly prized are the many varieties of mutant snail – such as the luridly-colored jewelspiral varieties, and the so-called "flailing snail" – a spike-crowned beast.

Located in the upper reaches of towers to protect grain from rats, the city's **granaries** are typically surrounded by prides of the snow-white breed of **granary cat** characteristic of Vornheim. Small, unassuming, vicious and surprisingly intelligent, they're immune to poison and disease and can climb almost vertically down ice-laced stone.

Vornheim is home to a dizzying variety of **festivals** but only two are celebrated throughout the entire city: the **Day of Masks,** where everyone must wear a disguise (which supposedly fools the Demon of the Eightfold Wind into believing Vornheim is another city entirely and therefore ignoring it), and the **Day of Wolves**, where the citizens leave freshly-slain goats in the alleys, abandon the streets, and throw open the gates of the city to the wolves. The citizens then move from place to place using only bridges and underground walkways. Any wolves remaining the next morning are slain and roasted.

It is known to some scholars that the **skins of all snakes can be read like books.** Those who speak the serpent language know that these creatures continuously hiss their titles. As they grow, the animals revise and expand themselves, shedding old knowledge for new. The most common and convenient method of reading a snake (among human ophidobibliologists) is to have it slither through an ivory serpent-reader – a sphere with ornately carved orifices and channels. Common snakes are usually fairly uninteresting works – garter snakes tend to be cookbooks, corn snakes are generally works of adventure fiction with cliche characters or too-convenient endings. Rarer breeds – 100' anacondas, albino cobras – often contain long-forgotten secrets or comprise unique works of poetry or philosophy.

Giant snakes are typically encyclopedias or great multi-volume sagas representing the myths and theogonies of entire cultures. Nagas are linguistic texts, translating from the languages of snakes to the languages of humans. The snakes growing from the heads of medusae are generally reference works and the medusae themselves are often cataloguers

In Vornheim

– tending private libraries containing nothing but caged snakes, selectively breeding exotic and daring new works. The Librarians – also known as serpent men – also catalogue and breed books, though in a far less dilettantish and casual fashion – they believe that careful control of cross-species breeding can and will one day unveil a Great Glistening Book containing all the secrets of creation.

It is said that beneath every great library in human civilization a cabal of wizard-scholars tends to a chained Lernean Hydra. These scholars carefully transcribe and translate the information gleaned from the beast's skin before pruning off each head in turn and reading what grows in its place, thereby nurturing a constantly updated stream of knowledge.

Dragons are books of magic spells. Owing to the difficulty of reading them while alive, complete dragon hides will almost always fetch a higher price from the right sorcerer or alchemist than from any armorer. Minidragons are helpful but incomplete summaries of the contents of their larger brethren. Scholars disagree: the amphisbaena is either a palindrome or a work which reveals an entirely different (yet equally coherent) narrative when read backwards. The skins of snake-demons contain horrible secrets and blasphemies...

In the center of the square between the Palace Massive and Eminent Cathedral, there is a well. At the bottom of the well lives The Wyvern, who is both wealthy and wise. For reasons now lost to history, each citizen of Vornheim has the right – once in life – to climb down into the well and demand the answer to one question from the **Wyvern of the Well**. In exchange for this (always correct) answer, the Wyvern demands 700 gold pieces and will, in turn, ask the inquirer one question. What the Wyvern does with the answers thus accumulated from the people of Vornheim (or the gold, for that matter), or why it – being, apparently, omniscient – bothers to ask, is unknown.

Naturally, the questions asked of the Wyvern tend to be personal, local, and, of course, petty. It is conjectured that the Wyvern, knowing – as a consequence of its ancient, strange contract or curse – the innermost hearts of the people of Vornheim, despises them for the myopic schemers they are.

However, no-one wants to spend their one question asking it.

Some speculate that the Wyvern is cursed to know nothing except the answers to whatever questions the people of Vornheim will one day ask and what they tell him. In which case it is likely that the Wyvern went mad long ago.

The Chain is not – as is widely supposed – an ancient death cult, but a pair of long-lived humunculi who devour the minds of innocents, reside in their skulls, and use their bodies to carry out assassinations for pay. Once a contract is accepted, the humunculi of The Chain will not stop, and will attack from any available body until their quarry is slain – often pursuing a target for decades. If a host is slain, the humunculus will generally exit through the eyesocket (leaving the empty skull to collapse) and crawl quickly off to occupy a new host.

Three ancient witches live secretly in Vornheim – grey-haired **Thorn**, who is served by wild animals and creeping plants, black-haired **Dread** – an illusionist and a deceiver – and pale-haired **Frost** – mistress of numb, cold and frozen things. They roam the city disguised as young women, with their familiars (wolf, raven and white owl, respectively) likewise disguised. They scheme to subvert all human rule, summon the **Ring Wolf** – a circular demon, who takes a form like a rolling wheel of coarse fur with wolves' heads radiating from the rim – and enthrone Belphegor, Lord of Beasts.

Other **demons** reported to the Church of Vorn include one with the head of a boar, the body of a bloated man and the legs of a spider, a bipedal goat with a toothed mouth embedded in its stomach, covered in frost, and a man with the face of a crow wearing a hood and carrying a hooked blade. Such creatures are seldom seen inside the city walls, yet their influence is much feared.

In addition to the entries in the standard bestiary, naturalists of Vornheim have identified the following rare and unusual species:

To the untutored eye, a **Hollow Bride** appears to be an ordinary woman wearing a floor-length dress with her arms dangling limply at her sides. In actuality, a Bride has no body and consists of nothing more than a pair of hands fixed at the wrist to the ends of the empty sleeves of an empty dress held erect by a floating, vampiric head. The dress maintains its shape through the action of animated entrails dangling from the thing's neck and, occasionally, with the aid of corset-like boning sewn into the garment. In combat, the hands can break free and operate independently. These pitiable undead Brides long to mix with the living and cannot refuse invitations to social gatherings of any kind.

A **Thornchild** is a creature with the body of an enormous serpentine rose with the head of an elven child nestled amid the petals. Though anchored to the ground, they drag their coiling, spiked bodies through cities, forests, and wild gardens by means of spindly, clawed-tipped arms. Witches and druids are known to be able to summon them.

An Eye of Fate consists of a small snake's body surmounted by a dead thief's hand, with the eye of a lunatic or a blind man set into the palm. They are a kind of evil humunculus created by witches of the northern wastes, who employ them to spy on their foes and, occasionally, to suffocate them in their sleep. The eye set into the withered palm acts as both a scrying device and a weapon. If the creature was made using a blind eye, then anyone gazing into the eye must save or be blinded. If the creature was made using a maniac's eye then the victim must save or go temporarily mad. If slain, the creature turns into a glove. The glove will fit no-one except the witch who sent the Eye, and will fit her in whatever guise she may adopt.

Maggot (or Grub) Nagas are uncanny things with the heads of beautiful women and bloated, white, wormlike bodies. They range from three to six feet in length, and are as likely to be found conversing in the meeting halls of great houses as nesting in the digestive tracts of aging dragons. Whether these unsettling creatures are related to true nagas is unclear, but they exhibit similar abilities – albeit on a lesser scale – and an even more frightening intelligence. Their council is much prized in certain rarefied circles, for they possess unusual insight into the science of governance.

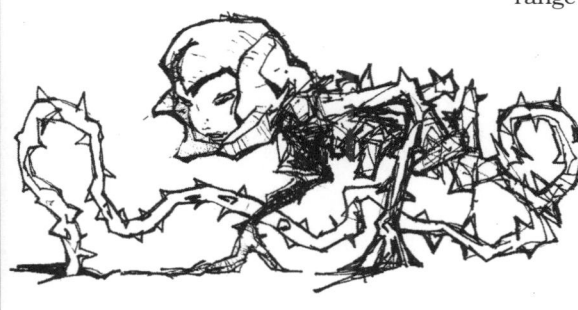

Superstitions of Vornheim

Long lines of inconceivably corrupt rulers have used their city as a bargaining chip in any number of agreements, compromises, and alliances with a wide variety of deities, demons, and esoteric entities over the centuries, with the result that the citizens go about their lives enmeshed in an dense weave of restraining and sustaining taboos. Which beliefs are accurate and which are in error is left entirely to the individual GMs, since they can be difficult to keep track of.

- The number 6 is lucky in Vornheim. Any member of a party with 6 members will succeed on a d20 roll if they roll a 6 once per day (or session – GM's discretion).
- The number 7 is unlucky in Vornheim. Any member of a party with 7 members will fail spectacularly on a roll of 7 once per day (or session – GM's discretion).
- If a granary cat crosses your path and you don't feed it, your food will taste bitter for 7 days – save vs poison to manage to eat any meal.
- The color brown is reserved by Vorn, to use on rust. Anyone going outdoors wearing brown is pelted with snow by children until the cloth is no longer visible. Southerners whose skin is brown are considered blessed and are looked upon with awe.

Superstitions of Vornheim

- Blunt weapons are forbidden to clerics of Vorn as they are signs of hypocrisy. "If thou wouldst bring harm, bring it" sayeth he. Clerics using any unpointed weapon (including a fist) will lose a spell that day (or the next if they are all spent).
- If a hunter desires to kill a stag, s/he must do it alone and without a bow, or the meat will putrefy.
- If an animal is tracked from Vornheim to its home and then slain by a hunter with his/her bare hands, and then the animal's blood is poured into all the tracks, and the hunter drinks the blood from all these tracks, s/he will become a werewolf.
- A child must not sleep in stripes, or else it will be replaced with a doppleganger in the night.
- Among the nobility it is believed that the first thing a child must taste is a tiny drop of poison, or else it will die by poison in old age.
- The sea gods mistrust Vornheim. Any native must sacrifice a stag before sailing or face great difficulty at sea.
- It is forbidden to plant a tree where a tree once was. (The shadows of missing trees persist in Vornheim for months after the trees themselves are removed.)
- If someone tries to kill a snake without introducing him/herself to the snake first, the snake will be poisonous.
- In the southeastern district, if a criminal is publicly executed and no-one laughs, everyone present will lose a family member within the year. (The constabulary therefore goes to great lengths to devise humorous methods of execution.)
- No-one can die in a room so long as the room contains a toad in a bowl. The toad must be alive, remain of its own accord, and cannot be bound in any way to the bowl, physically, by magic, or by persuasion. The charm fails if there is more than one toad in the room.
- Cows are considered indolent and undesirable. Anyone bringing a live cow into Vornheim will lose a shoe within the week.
- If someone sneezes, everyone present must pretend to sneeze, or else the sneezer will be possessed by a demon whose power is relative to the sneezer's station.
- Whaleflesh is prized. Anyone bringing an entire adult whale into the city and distributing the meat freely will be lord of the city for 5 days.
- A rat in a tavern must be killed with a dagger, a dart, an axe, or by a cat – but never by poison, or else the floor will rot away within the month.
- Anyone buying a hat for a fisherman will be struck dumb for 3 days.
- Anyone seeing a wolf must drink a toast to it that night, or more will come.
- If a wolf sits upon the throne, all men will weep, the moon will darken, and all children will turn away from their parents.
- All cakes must be tasted by the oldest person in the room first, or else they will taste like fish. Except fishcakes, which will taste like rye.
- To appease the gods of night and of the moon – who wield special influence in Vornheim – the first thing citizens must do upon seeing the sun is curse it. Otherwise they will be unable to hear music for three days.
- No dog will be faithful to someone who gives leftovers to a crow.
- A pregnant woman must never drink alcohol – if she does, a vampire will wake her after she falls asleep and ask if it can take her child. In her disoriented condition she will agree.
- If a sister objects to a wedding, it is invalid.
- If someone is murdered in the city, their skull must be split in half before they are buried or else a succubus will incubate in its skull and rise from the grave, fully formed, after 17 days.
- No lord or regent of the city may touch, harm or in any way restrain a snow leopard, else s/he will die of a leopard-spot pox the next day.
- Pigs must be present during all trials.

House of the Medusa Introduction

Once, demons ruled every universe, unchecked. Then came 12 sisters – medusae – they looked upon the demon kings and changed them to stone, and drove the rest away. The grey bones of this earth were hewn from the petrified bodies of these demon kings. Or at least that's what the 12 sisters will tell you.

At any rate, though masked and monstrous, the twelve sisters are respected in all nations. One of the most civilized of the sisters – Eshrigel – has long lived in Vornheim.

Despite her position as a wealthy pillar of Vornheim society, Eshrigel cares for no-one but herself, nothing but her own comfort, and is, in truth, a Machiavellian survivor and the author of a thousand cruelties, eager for...well, whatever. It's your campaign, you motivate the NPCs. Point is, if your campaign needs a decadent, sociopathic schemer (and whose doesn't?), there you go. I had her plotting with goblins so she could assassinate the Wyvern of the Well and read all the secrets off his skin.

If your campaign progresses to the point where the PCs decide they want to try to slay her in her own home, find evidence of her crimes, or if they just need a luxurious house to rob, here it is...

The house is modestly-sized and is not in a tower, though it is in a well-to-do neighborhood and residents will notice any trouble.

Difficulty: The house is suitable for PCs of level 1 – 4 *with few or no powerful magic items*, though success rates depend more on how prepared the PCs are than anything else. If the PCs don't know they're entering a medusa's house, it'll be considerably more difficult.

Due to the magic windows and impenetrable doors, half the challenge will be simply trying to find a way in.

Details (map on page 12)

Eshrigel will answer the front door (wearing her mask) if anyone knocks during daylight hours. She will look out the window first, to make sure they are neither armed nor armored. Otherwise she'll be in a randomly determined room (Where's Eshrigel?, page 13).

If she receives her visitors, she will usually bring them to the parlor where the Plasmic Ghoul will appear to be safely caged. She will entertain guests cordially.

During social functions, she and her guests will be served by blind, albino slaves. Statwise, they are identical to Gudge (pg 23).

The rugs and other furnishings in any room are worth d10 x 10 gp each but any dealer in Vornheim will know where they came from.

The **Plasmic Ghoul** lives in room N on the first floor, but has excellent hearing and will seek out the source of any loud noises or vibrations anywhere in the house. Eshrigel will usually let the ghoul deal with intruders if it finds them first.

If Eshrigel is slain, all the statues will come to life. Their details are left to the GM. If the myths are true, about 1/12 of the stone on the planet (and 1/12th of the planet itself) should revert to flesh upon her death. The GM may interpret this how s/he wishes.

How vulnerable the walls are to magic, explosives, superhuman strength, etc. is left to the GM.

The **windows** are made from demons magically turned to glass. **First floor windows** are unbreakable. **Second floor windows** are breakable from the inside and unbreakable from the outside.

A Stone cupola on roof.
(The cupola is shown from the side on the map, unlike the other rooms, which are shown from above, as usual). **Door** is locked and requires Str 21 to force open. The hand-shaped doorknob will come alive and grab the hand of anyone other than Eshrigel who tries to open the door or pick the lock. Its grip is unbreakable. The lock can be picked, however.

B Study
Chair, desk. Any special information on Eshrigel's schemes the PCs may be looking for is here.

C Secret statue room
Contains d10 + 10 victims of Eshrigel that she prefers not to display publicly in room M. A variety of sentient species are represented as well as a few celebrated and high-level missing persons. **If Eshrigel is slain**, they will return to life – confused. It will take them some time to find the secret door and escape (the door is secret in both directions).

D Child's bedroom
Belongs to Medusa's daughter, Absalom (whereabouts unknown). Her remaining toys (stuffed bear, jack-in-the-box, wooden duck, etc.) have been animated – they are harmless in themselves but act as an alarm system and will make enough noise to alert Eshrigel to the presence of anyone entering the room.

E Library
Walls lined with a grid of 200 1' x 1' cages set into the walls, 2' deep, each containing an ordinary snake. In the center of the room is a snake-reader on a lectern with a magnifying glass attached. (see Snakes as Books pg 7)

F Eshrigel's bedroom
If Eshrigel is not in this room the (ordinary) doors will be locked. **Secret door**: behind a large painting of a battle (in a style reminiscent of Paolo Uccello) – a thin crack will be visible if the painting is moved and a successful check (secret door check, perception check, etc.) is made. Room contains a make-up table (no mirror, of course), a canopy bed hung with velvet, d12 x 100 gp worth of jewelry. The bed, painting, Eshrigel's wardrobe, and the table are each worth d12 x 100 gp but any dealer in the city will know who they belong to. There is a **small box** with a poison needle trap under the bed containing 600 gp and a locket with a small painting of Eshrigel and her daughter (unmasked) inside. How the painting was successfully executed is unclear.

G Hallway
There is a **cursed dictionary of psychological ailments** lying open on a lectern. Any creature inspecting it (and able to read the local common tongue) will be afflicted by an illness. Roll on the table on page 15.

H Water closet
(No mirror.)

I Dining room
Table is usually set. If Eshrigel is in this room she will be eating and her mask will be off. Three paintings here: each eight feet wide, worth 2,000 gp each, though any dealer in Vornheim will know where they came from.

J Music room
There is (anachronistically) a grand piano here worth 2,500 gp (it's not easy to move). The **Plasmic Ghoul** hates piano music and will not enter or remain in the room if it is being played.

K Kitchen
Pots, pans, the usual. There is a brick oven and a small **pantry closet**. A halfling could fit in it.

L Entry hall
11 small portrait paintings. One of each of Eshrigel's sisters (including Thrace pg 23). They are worth d20 x 100 gp to collectors with unusual tastes, but any dealer will know where they came from.

M Statue room
10 statues of Eshrigel's victims – thieves (d4 level) caught breaking into the house and a pair of notorious criminals (Eshrigel's rivals) – Torga the Hideous and Vorzhak Rakk (9th level thieves).

N Parlor
2 sofas, a long, low table, a life – sized sculpture of a hand in jade (worth 400gp), a hookah, a chandelier, a **statue** of a thief (1st level), a cage hanging from the ceiling containing the **Plasmic Ghoul** (not locked).

Other Notes:
- The Ghoul will seek out any loud noises or vibrations.
- Furnishings in a typical room are worth d10 x d10 gp.
- If Eshrigel is slain, the statues come to life.
- First floor windows are unbreakable.
- Second floor windows are unbreakable from the outside.

Where's Eshrigel	
d20	
1	A
2-3	B
4	C
5	D
6-7	E
8-9	F
10	G
11	H
12-13	I
15-15	J
16-17	K
18	M
19-20	N

Plasmic Ghoul

A transparent ooze, 5 gallons in volume, surmounted by a lolling, rolling, zombie-like head.

HD: 5 **Speed**: as human
AC: 8 or 12 **Intelligence**: animal

Attack: Touch (d10hp and dissolves d10 AC worth of metal armor per successful attack). Ignores AC from metal armor when attacking.

Defense: Turns as a mummy. Immune to non – magical attacks.

Eshrigel the Medusa

6' tall woman with snakes instead of hair. If ripped out, the 8 snakes on Eshrigel's head can be read like any other snake. They are spellbooks containing one 8th level spell each, usable as a scroll (if the reader uses a snake-reader). They will be illegible if she is petrified.

HD: 8 **Speed**: as human
AC: 5 or 15 **Intelligence**: 17
(high dexterity)

Attack: Gaze attack – save vs. paralysis or be petrified until Eshrigel dies. Target's eyes must meet hers. If she petrifies herself the effect is permanent. If she's petrified that counts as "dead". Poisoned throwing dagger (d4 + save vs. poison or *Sleep* spell-like effect) if gaze attack is for some reason impractical.

Cursed dictionary

Appears to be an ordinary handbook of psychological ailments, but examining it causes madness.

Roll below (effects last 10 minutes, unless victim enters combat, in which case they last only a further d6 rounds):

1. Target becomes a kleptomaniac.
2. Target has a 50% chance of doing exactly the opposite of whatever s/he wants to do after declaring any action.
3. Target needs a strong drink before taking any action.
4. Target attacks nearest friendly PC.
5. Target believes s/he is nearest friendly PC.
6. Target is paralyzed with indecision.
7. Target has to roll on this chart once each round.
8. Target thinks s/he is dead.
9. Target thinks s/he is nearest foe.
10. Target becomes obsessed with nearby irrelevant object.
11. Target runs to window and tries to jump out.
12. Target drops his/her weapon and begins to cry loudly for help in any and all languages known to him/her.

Immortal Zoo of Ping Feng Introduction

When, exactly, astrologer and animal-lover Ping Feng settled in Vornheim – and in what quarter – has been debated for centuries. Scholars generally agree, however, that his baffling zoo did exist, and that the many strange and wondrous animals contained therein were indeed immune to death by old age. A vocal minority claim they live still, and that their home lies intact somewhere – bricked up, buried, or simply disguised beneath the ancient layers of built, rebuilt, and overbuilt towers that make up Vornheim.

They're right. The magic that keeps the zoo animals alive has also subtly worked to preserve and hide the zoo itself.

When Ping Feng died, his manservant Gudge was bound by sorcery to protect the animals forever. Although Gudge still lives in the zoo, one of the animals – a nightingale – ate his mind while he was sleeping, 200 years ago. This turned Gudge into a hollow automaton and transferred mystic responsibility for the zoo to the nightingale.

The nightingale occasionally leaves the zoo, sometimes in the company of Gudge – to make deals, often through proxies, for shiny objects or meals (rare insects and worms, mostly), and occasionally carries out more enigmatic errands.

Many have gone in search of the zoo, drawn by curiosity, the value of its rare animals, and the promise of discovering the secrets of immortality.

The zoo itself is a dungeon that can be placed anywhere in the city the GM likes – it could be in a completely forgotten corner, or it could have been secretly preserved or unearthed by a powerful NPC.

This is, at its heart, a hack-n-slash adventure that requires solving a puzzle to get out of it. It should, however, not be so much next-room-next-monster as a strategic cat-and-mouse game where the GM has control of several cats.

Difficulty: Although this location's designed for PCs of 4th – 7th level *with few, if any, magic items*, the most crucial factor is how experienced and/or clever the players and/or GM are. If the players quickly realize the nightingale is the Master, a group of 1st level PCs could crack it. Having more players will probably help, no matter what level they are. If the GM carefully disguises the nightingale among red herring details and plays the nightingale tactically – releasing multiple monsters to attack PCs from behind while they're already engaged, etc., the Zoo could challenge any group. Another important factor is preparation – if the PCs go into the zoo knowing what it is and the kinds of dangers it contains, the Zoo will be far easier to survive than if they stumble on it and only realize what it is after they've begun exploring.

Note: Because of space limitations in this book, the Zoo has been designed as a mostly self-contained interior location-based adventure in order to provide a simple mechanism for the animals to be set free and fight the PCs: The nightingale has to free the animals in order to protect the zoo because it has no other resources to fight with.

However, a GM willing to put some effort into devising a more plot-based adventure (an earthquake, an animal liberation cult, a thief trying to cause a distraction, etc.) could easily create a version of the zoo that is not forgotten and hidden but is more of an integrated part of the city. If you'd like to go this route, the zoo could be placed in Zorlac or Eshrigel's basement or even – with well-designed guards and fences – outdoors. Finding a reason and a way to trap the PCs inside will help make it fun, but if your PCs are greedy or crazy enough to want to steal one of the more dangerous animals you won't have to trap them to make the Zoo into an interesting challenge.

Such a "living" version of the zoo would probably contain food for all the animals, including: gems to feed the xortoise, living humans and monkeys to feed Parnival and Vorkuta, respectively, swarms of exotic or magical insects to feed the toad and peacock (possibly spawn of the demonic fly), and the souls of the pure of heart (or recently corrupted) to feed the goatscorpion, peryton, and demonic fly.

Immortal Zoo of Ping Feng Details

The Zoo has a lonely and only slightly dilapidated beauty. The walls are covered in inch-square tiles of jade, lapis, and marble (worth its weight in gold, but the nightingale will object to such vandalism). The sound of the octopus' fountain is audible throughout. The ceilings are 40' high, the walls are unbreakable – except by magic, but the ceilings aren't. 10' archways separate halls from rooms. If the xortoise is slain, the walls are vulnerable to magic that affects earth and stone, though this will in no way be obvious. There are torches in sconces every 10' in every room except the Supply Room.

Most of the animals (except as noted on the map key) are in ornate magical cages which prevent them from using any supernatural abilities on visitors so long as the animals are caged. There is a nameplate (in an ancient dialect) next to each cage accompanied by a set of sliding tiles that can be used to open or close the cage (the nameplates contain no information of value). The cages are 10' x 10' unless otherwise noted.

Sliding tiles also open all the (non-secret) doors.

As soon as the PCs enter, the front gate will close immediately and it cannot be opened by any ordinary means or standard magic (if the PCs manage to lodge something in it before it closes, it's up to the GM whether that'll hold the door open.) A wizard will recognize the gate as a "Master Door" that will open only at the request of a single master.

At this point the nightingale will go to work (see below).

None of the intelligent animals will willingly aid the PCs except the griffon unless offered something valuable in return (other than their freedom – most are too insane, content with their immortality, or suspicious of humans to care about being set free all by itself). Aside from the griffon, none know the nightingale is in charge. All are hungry, since they've eaten only sporadically over the last millennia and will try to eat the PCs.

The magic that keeps the animals immortal will fade if they are removed from the zoo – they will live out their normal lifespans and then die.

The animals are worth 2 times their XP value in gold (unless otherwise noted) if they can be sold alive to the right collector. The oblique projection used on the map displays north-south distances as shorter than east-west ones, the scales running along the top and sides of the map reflect this. Animals, doors, and stairs are not to scale on the map, they're just drawn that way to make it easier for the GM to help the nightingale plan where it wants to go relative to the PCs.

PCs enter on the bottom.

Any area not keyed is empty, perhaps containing a broken cage.

Except as noted, the secret doors will yield to a standard-difficulty (active) check. They are unpickably locked and can only be opened by the key in the **Supply Room** but they can be forced open by the flailceratops.

Nightingale Triggers and Tactics	
If the Nightingale sees....	**It will secretly...**
PCs enter area B	Flee & begin to spy on PCs
PCs seem to be moving steadily north	Wait
PCs open a secret door	Release nearest dangerous monster
PCs enter NW hallway between areas R & W	Release nearest dangerous monster
PCs begin to turn back	Release nearest dangerous monster
PCs fighting a monster	Release nearest monster behind party
Party split	Release monster between halves of the party if possible
PCs defeating monsters handily	Release some or all of the most dangerous monsters simultaneously

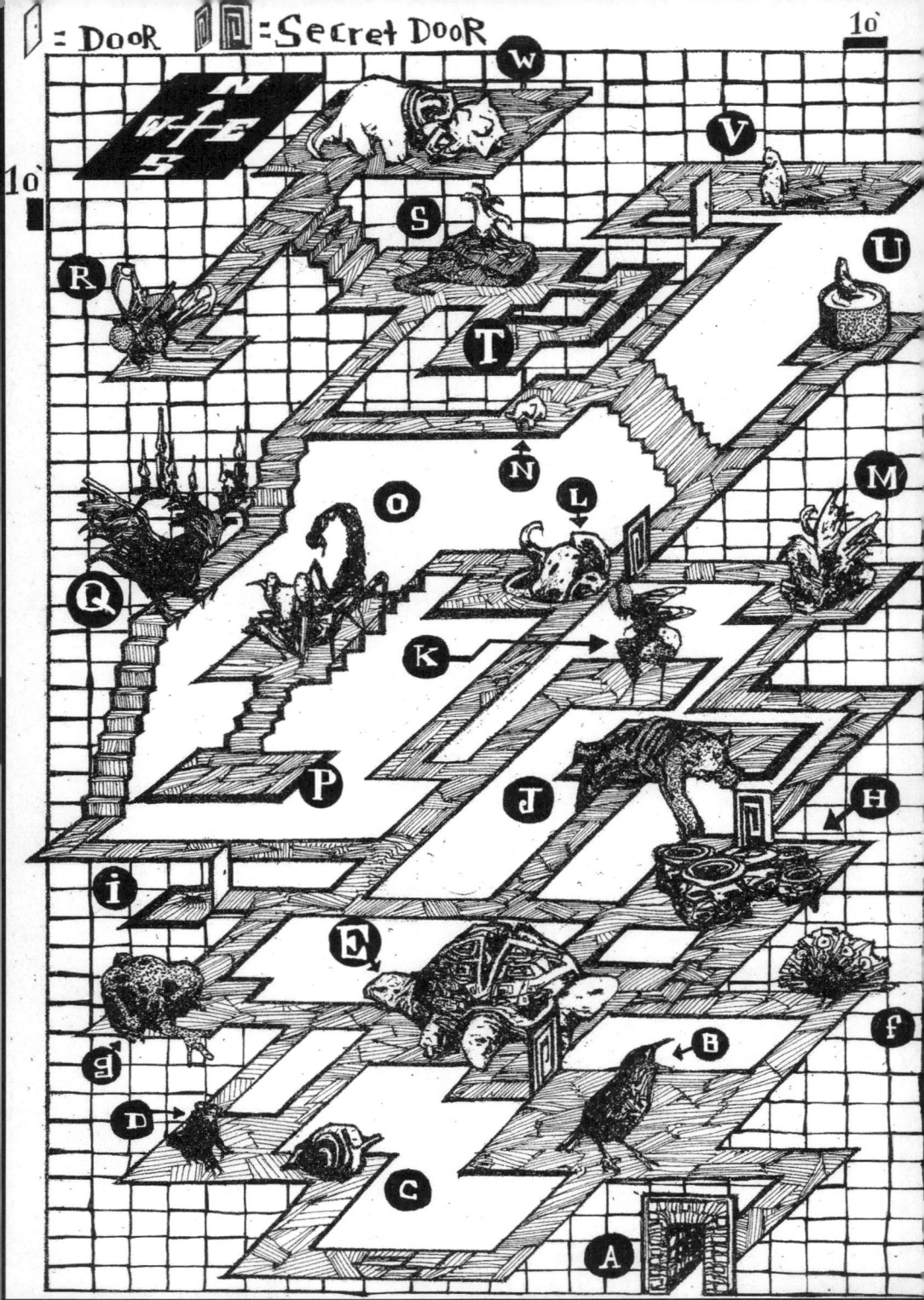

A Front Gate The 'Master Door' (see above). It can look however the GM wants on the outside. The inside is intricate and ornate.

B Roaming this area freely is the **Nightingale** – A small, unremarkable-looking bird. The nightingale will flee as soon as it sees any intruder (unless the party enters by magical means). The nightingale will automatically gain initiative the first time it sees the party – it can hear them coming.

C Roaming this area freely – crawling the walls – is a **Mutant Snail**. It is a foot tall and eerily beautiful, with a spiral shell of rich yellow and deep blue. It is harmless. If unmolested, it will continue to roam the halls. Worth 500 gp.

D Parnival, Vampire Monkey This colobus monkey is intelligent and can speak but remains quiet because it's afraid someone will force it to work. It is hungry for blood.

E Xortoise The four-headed, radially symmetrical xortoise's turtle-like shell is crisscrossed by a great x-shaped, spiketoothed mouth. It is 15' in diameter. Cage is 25' x 25'.

F Roaming this corridor freely is a **Narcissus Peacock**. It resembles an ordinary peacock – until it spreads its fan. If it is not slain here, it will continue to roam the halls randomly.

G Unsettling Toad a small and unnatural-looking beast. It does not communicate but can sing with the voice of a young girl.

H Mottled Fungi Gudge throws organic waste into this room where this brightly-colored fungi consumes it, as it long ago devoured whatever once lived in the ruined cage. The fungi covers the entire room, including the north wall, obscuring the secret door there. It is nonintelligent, but it can sense heat and will not attack until at least three creatures are standing in it. (Maybe less if there are fewer PCs in the party.)

I Water Closet

J Blue Tiger An extraordinarily rare animal from the mountain jungles of the far east.

K Firefly Woman Human-sized insect-like female with a bioluminescent thorax. She is harmless and wants only to return to wherever she came from (GM decides). She speaks an unknown language and her name is merely a series of clicks and hisses. Certain nobles with exotic tastes will pay handsomely for her.

L White Octopus 30 feet across, tiny mouths embedded in each sucker. The circular well in the cage is 15' across and 40' deep. If it is a moonless night, Raxia and Danica – two mad sisters from great houses who frolic with the octopus – will be visiting. The nightingale knows they are harmless and ordinarily lets them in and out at will. They possess no valuable information and the nightingale will not let them out while the PCs are in the Zoo.

M Ozwick, the Griffon His cage is littered with embroidered pillows and used teacups. He knows all about the nightingale, which is why the nightingale has had Gudge wall him up in a secret chamber and keeps him drunk on tea fortified with rum, white wine, and herbal liquer. He speaks most local languages, is a charming raconteur, and wishes to escape. However, he is hopelessly drunk, and will remain so for 8 hours and does not know how to open the front gate. Gudge will bring him enough tea to keep him drunk every 4 hours. He is too old to fight or fly and, if he escapes, will attempt to adopt a sedentary existence in mildly opulent surroundings.

N Miniphant This species of kitten-sized elephant is rare, docile, and harmless. Worth 600 gp.

O Goatscorpion Goat's head, giant scorpion's body. It despises innocence and will attack the most virtuous party member first.

P "Treasure" Room Once a garden, this room is littered with small, worthless shiny objects the nightingale has collected.

Q Candelabraxian Peryton Mysterious creature with the body of an eagle, breast and head of a stag, with 7 everburning candles entwined in its antlers. Its 7 overlapping shadows are those of men. All of Hell can be seen in the creature's left eye so long as it lives. The cage is set into the wall.

R Demonic Fly Huge insect body, head like a bug-eyed caricature of a human face. It is dumb and vicious, but has an intricate knowledge of politics.

S Thrace, the Nagadusa 20' long python's body, woman's head, smaller snakes instead of hair. Sister of Eshrigel, gone mad long ago. Cage is 15' cube. She may aid the PCs if they convince her they can help her escape but she will turn on them immediately after passing the front gate. She admires her sister, Eshrigel, and will make any deal to be reunited with her, but again, will turn on anyone aware of her existence immediately upon escaping.

T Empty cages may still have nameplates if the GM can think of something in time.

U Vorkuta, the Nephilidian (Amphibious) Vampire Floating palely in a small topless tank (5' across, 15' deep), Vorkuta is quite mad. She has gills in her neck and pale blue eyes. She babbles parts of old conversations and snatches of fairy tales. She will attack anyone who doesn't humor her, however, and will try to swallow any jewelry she sees.

V Supply room – brooms, shovels, etc. Gudge is here – a drooling, corpulent drone of a man in silk robes with pale, doughy skin. He does not speak and obeys the nightingale. The room is lit by a simple chandelier hanging 12 feet above the floor. Gudge has (as always) shoved the key to the secret doors into one of the candles at such a height that the candle will burn down and the key will fall to the floor exactly 4 hours after the last time Ozwick was fed.

W Flailceratops Product of cruel alchemical experimentation. It has the body of a triceratops (20' long), and an enormous spiked ball on a chain where its head should be. The cage is 25' x 30'.

Immortal Zoo of Ping Feng

Stats and Details

Nightingale

As soon as it is unseen, it will free the zoo animals, hoping they will kill the intruders. It will not perform any intelligent acts if it thinks an outsider can see it and so will only free zoo animals when out of sight of the party. It knows how to open all the cages and secret doors throughout the zoo, and will use the secret doors to circumvent or hide from intruders. The GM will probably want to keep track of where the nightingale is throughout the adventure. It can speak most local languages but only if forced to. It is the only creature that the front gate will open for, though it will not leave while intruders are in the zoo.

At first, it will hesitate to free more than one creature at a time, since getting them back into their cages is difficult, but it is smart enough to free more if the party proves to be a genuine threat (it likes to wait until the party is engaged with one monster, and then release another to sneak attack from behind). The nightingale is cunning and will wait until the PCs are deep into the Zoo (near the more dangerous animals on the north end of the map) before releasing animals – unless the PCs start causing trouble right away. It will let the PCs escape if it is captured and credibly threatened. If a PC eats its brain, s/he will take on the knowledge, responsibilities and personality of the animal.

HD: 1   **Speed**: as human
AC: 5 or 15   **Intelligence**: 18 (due to size and Dexterity)

Attack: Will not attack unless cornered and threatened, if so: casts *Suggestion* at will as if it were a 10th level wizard.

Mutant Snail
– It will eat only printed words beginning with the letter "S". HD: 1 Speed: 1/4 human AC: 9 or 11 Intelligence: Animal

Parnival, Vampire Monkey

HD: 4   **Speed**: as human
AC: 8 or 12   **Intelligence**: 9 (due to Dex)

Attack: Claw (d4hp) or grapple with 9 Strength – if successful, he may automatically bite the next round and will drain a level from his victim, adding 4 hit points for each level drained. If he successfully slays a victim in this way, it will become a vampire. It will be subject to Parnival's will until he is permanently slain. Whether the victim remains a vampire, dies, or returns to ordinary form depends on how goth the campaign is. Can climb into any deep shadow and emerge from any other within one mile as if through a tunnel.

Defense: If reduced to zero hit points within the zoo, Parnival will turn into a mobile pool of black blood and escape, regenerating 1hp per hour. A drop of blood from another vampire is sufficient to revive him fully. Sunlight or a stake through the heart will slay him permanently. Holy water causes 2 – 7hp damage. He is immune to poison. Turns as a vampire.

Xortoise

The markings on its shell comprise a text of great philosophical importance in an ancient language (GM's choice). Any wizard, cleric, or monk who learns the language (or uses magic to read it) and studies the intact shell for one month will gain enough experience to advance one level. Anyone braving the central mouth of the xortoise (bites for double normal damage) will find a pearl the size and weight of a small boulder worth 10,000 gp.

HD: 10   **Speed**: 1/3 human
AC: 0   **Intelligence**: animal
natural 19 or 20 to hit the xortoise does +10 damage

Attack: Up to 4 bites (d6 x 4hp each), but each bite must be at a different target.

Defense: It is impossible to flank or backstab the xortoise. As it is part earth elemental, spells controlling the earth have unpredictable effects when cast upon the xortoise.

Note: It's too large to fit through the tunnels surrounding its room by ordinary means. HOWEVER: if the Xortoise is uncaged and attempts to chase the PCs out of the room, its thrashings will cause the ceilings to weaken. If this happens there is a 50% chance per round that the ceiling in the hallway the xortoise is trying to get into will collapse, causing 3d10 damage to anyone anywhere in that hallway and completely blocking the archways on either end (i.e. anyone inside is trapped and the hallway's no longer usable until cleared out, which will take 300 minutes minus 1 per strength point of each creature helping clear the rubble). This will not produce a passable exit to the surface through the ceiling

Narcissus Peacock

HD: 2   **Speed**: as human

AC: 9 or 11   **Intelligence**: animal

Attack: Upon seeing any creature, the peacock will spread its fan. Creatures seeing it must save or stand immobile and transfixed. (Theories differ as to what, exactly, a victim sees when it gazes into the tailfeathers – when a PC is frozen, ask the player what s/he sees). The peacock will then begin to eat the victim(s), causing d4 pecking damage per round. Victims may make another save every time they take damage. The effect ends if the beast is slain.

Unsettling Toad

This small toad is so disturbing to look at that its victims go blind. It cannot speak but can sing with the voice of a young girl.

HD: 4   **Speed**: 2x human

AC: 8 or 12   Intelligence: animal (due to Dexterity)

Attack: Save vs. spell or go blind for 2 days.

Mottled Fungi

Any creature attempting to move through it moves at half speed.

HD: 4   **Speed**: the fungi is immobile, but it completely coats the room and the tunnel passing it.

AC: 7 or 13   **Intelligence**: None

Attack: Lashing tendril – save vs. poison or become infected. The infection makes the victim feel intoxicated and will begin to fully incubate in two (rounds/minutes/hours/days – roll d4). Full incubation causes a random body part to distend, distort, and pulse with lurid colors beneath the skin. All nearby carnivorous creatures will attack the victim. Also: The victim's allies will have to make a successful wisdom check every hour to recognize the victim – otherwise they will be unable to recognize the victim for who s/he truly is and will believe s/he is a stranger.

Blue Tiger

Anyone dreaming of a blue tiger will be attacked by one the following day.

HD: 6   **Speed**: 1.25xhuman

AC: 6 or 14   **Intelligence**: animal

Attack: 3 attacks: 2 claws (d4+1hp) and a bite (d10). If the first two claws hit, the tiger may make two additional claw attacks in the same round.

Defense: The tiger has 2 souls, so all spells must be cast twice to have any effect on it.

Firefly Woman HD: 2 Speed: as human on land or flying AC: 10 Intelligence: 10

White Octopus

(note that it can walk on land and will do so to look for food)

HD: 9   **Speed**: as human (in water) 1/3 human (on land)

AC: 7 or 13   **Intelligence**: animal

Attack: 6 tentacle attacks. Each does d10 damage from bites plus it can simultaneously attempt to disarm a foe, entangle a limb, or grapple an enemy as if it had a 16 Dexterity and a Strength of 15.

Note: The octopus has a 12' reach. It can survive outside of water for about an hour.

Raxia and Danica are 1HD humans. Wisdom: 3 Charisma: 12+ d6 Intelligence: 4

Ozwick, the Griffon HD: 7 Speed: As human AC: 5 or 15 Intelligence: 14 Charisma: 18

Miniphant HD: 1 Speed: as dog AC: 10 Intelligence: animal Attack: gore for d4 – 1

Immortal Zoo of Ping Feng

Stats and Details

Goatscorpion
(the demon's true name is unknown, but this name is descriptive)

HD: 8 **Speed**: 1.25x human

AC: 3 or 17 **Intelligence**: animal

Attack: 2 pincer attacks per round (d10hp) + spit vile black fluid range:10 ft (d6hp +d6 per selfless deed victim has performed in the last week) If the pincer attack is successful or if the attack would have been successful ignoring AC from armor (but not dex, magic, etc.) make an opposed strength roll: target rolls d12 + Str and goatscorpion rolls d12 + 15. If the goatscorpion then rolls highest, the victim is grabbed and the goatscorpion can make an extra attack the next round against the grabbed target: bite (d8hp), sting (save vs poison or take 10d6hp), or grab with the other pincer. If the victim survives, continue making opposed strength rolls at the end of each round to see if the victim escapes. If two victims are grabbed, the goatscorpion can only attempt to sting 1 per round. The goatscorpion rolls d12 + 18 on the opposed strength rolls if a single victim is grabbed with both pincers.

*Defense: See below.)

Note: If the goatscorpion is made to sting itself, it is vulnerable to its own poison.

Candelabraxian Peryton

Inside each of its candles is a small gem of a mysterious greenish – black substance worth 1000 gp and possessing bizarre alchemical qualities, however the gems will only be revealed if the candles are re – lit after the creature is slain and allowed to burn down – snapping them open reveals nothing.

HD: 9 **Speed**: as human
                    2x human (flying)

AC: 2 or 18 **Intelligence**: 5

Attack: claw (4 – 16hp) or gore (1 – 8hp plus ongoing magical fire damage: 1 – 6hp until the flames are extinguished as the candles – see below)

*Defense: It has 36 hit points, 28 of which reside in its 7 mystic candles. The only way to destroy those hit dice is to snuff out the candles. A candle is snuffed out if it takes more than 4 hp worth of damage from magically manipulated water or wind or is smothered in magically manipulated earth. The candles will also be extinguished if they are somehow deprived of oxygen for 4 rounds. The peryton's remaining hit die can be destroyed normally. The peryton gains an extra candle (and 4 extra hit points) every time it kills a humanoid.

Demonic Fly
(the demon's true name is unknown, but the demonic fly name is descriptive.)

HD: 8 **Speed**: ½ human
                  2x human (flying)

AC: 7 or 13 **Intelligence**: 10
                             (insane, does not speak)

Attack: 2 claws (d8hp each) or emit a sound causing collective hallucinations (all PCs hallucinate the same thing) (no save) to all within 10' for d4 rounds. GM should not tell players they are hallucinating and hallucinations will generally be of things that would cause the PCs to expend resources (water, spells, arrows, etc.) to "destroy" them or things which would make them remove their armor. The hallucinations will not obscure the presence of the demonic fly, though they may distort

* **The demonic fly**, **candelabraxian peryton** and **goatscorpion** are native to the lower planes of existence: They are immune to poison, flame and fear (unless the fear effect emanates from a good-alinged cleric). Spell attacks from casters with fewer levels than the creatures in question has HD have a 50% chance of failing.

it. A saving throw is allowed only if the player realizes the PC is hallucinating. The GM may provide such (small) clues as to the unreality of the hallucinations as s/he sees fit.

Defense: Takes half damage from weather or elemental attacks.

Thrace, the Nagadusa

HD: 11   **Speed**: as human

AC: 5 or 15   **Intelligence**: 12 (but insane)

Attack: 2 attacks per round: (1) Gaze attack – save vs. paralysis or be petrified until Thrace dies. Target's eyes must meet hers. If she petrifies herself the effect is permanent. (2) Constriction – Thrace rolls to hit, ignoring AC from armor (but not Dexterity, magic, etc.). If successful, target rolls d12 + Strength and Thrace rolls d12 + 17, if Thrace's total is higher, she does hp damage equal to the difference between the two modified rolls.

Note: If she is paralyzed by her own gaze, that counts as death. If the myths are true, about 1/12 of the stone on the planet (and 1/12th of the planet itself) should revert to flesh upon her death. The GM may interpret this however s/he wishes.

Vorkuta, the Nephilidian(Amphibious) Vampire

(equally at home in water or on land)

HD: 7   **Speed**: as human
                       2x human (swimming in fish form)

AC: 10   **Intelligence**: 9

Attack: Claw (d6hp) or grapple w/14 Strength – if successful, she may automatically bite the next round and will drain a level from her victim, adding its class levels and hit points to her own. If she successfully slays a victim in this way, it will become a nephilidian vampire. It will be subject to Vorkuta's will until she is permanently slain. Whether the victim remains a vampire, dies, or returns to ordinary form depends on how goth the campaign is.

Defense: She can transform into a small, mobile pool of black blood, or an aquatic form resembling a hybrid of a lionfish and a manta ray. If reduced to zero hit points within the zoo, Vorkuta will revert to the former form and escape, regenerating 1hp per hour. If grievously wounded in the water, Vorkuta will turn into sixteen black stones and sink to the bottom. In either form, a drop of blood from another vampire is sufficient to revive her completely. Sunlight or a stake through the heart will slay her permanently. Holy water causes 2 – 7hp damage. She is immune to poison and all forms of mind control. Turns as a vampire.

Gudge HD: 1 Speed: as human AC: 10 Intelligence: 3 Attack: improvised weapon at – 1 to hit (if ordered to attack)

Flailceratops

HD: 16   **Speed**: human

AC: 6 or 14   **Intelligence**: animal

Attack: Stomp (d12hp) or tail sweep (d12hp) or it may stand on its hind legs and swing the spiked ball at any target in front of it (3 – 36 hp). It can break down the master door if it can be made to constantly attack it for 10 minutes and the xortoise is dead.

Note: It's so wide it can only move at half speed through any corridor south or east of the Nagadusa's cage(Room S), though its AC from the front is effectively 3 steps better in such a situation. The ceilings are high enough to allow it to swing the ball at any target in front of it.

Library of Zorlac

Library of Zorlac

The five-towered home of Zorlac the Philosopher is widely known to contain one of the finest private collections of books in Vornheim. What is not generally known is that Zorlac is a compulsive bibliomaniac who builds his collection by employing a dozen well-paid scholar/thieves.

They are charged with acquiring any and all books from any promising target in or around Vornheim. If a book is not already in the library, it is stolen, and, if necessary, the owner is slain. These operatives double as librarians, each charged with organizing and curating one section of the collection.

Zorlac trusts no-one. Each librarian can only access his or her own section – through a series of secret doors hidden within the alcoves and spires of the library. Each is forbidden to use any entrance but their own. The magical oaths they take upon entering Zorlac's service prevent them from aiding, recognizing, or even noticing one another unless the library is breached by outsiders. He has them killed and replaced every few years to prevent any one scholar from becoming too intimate with the workings of the library.

Zorlac does not carry keys, for fear one of his thieves will steal them. Instead, he has installed secret doors activated by secret triggers he thinks only he knows.

Like many great libraries, Zorlac's has a hydra in the basement. Hired scholar-mages periodically prune and read the hydra's heads to keep abreast of recent artistic and scientific developments. (see Snake Books pg 7)

The Library can be treated as an adventure location or simply as a feature of the city – it does not necessarily have to be entered and "cleared" in order for Zorlac and his librarians to participate in a campaign in an interesting way.

PCs can come into contact with the library by any number of means – they could be mugged by a librarian for any books they might have, they could be asked to investigate such a theft, they could be told that a certain piece of information they want can probably only be found in the library, they could be invited to a social function at Zorlac's home and see one of the librarians skulking about, they could hear legends about The Oblong Rug, or the library could just be a resource that the PCs know is there. Since, in all likelihood, the PCs will be able to leave the library as soon as trouble arises, it's helpful for the PCs to have a built-in reason to investigate further.

In order to devise interesting adventures involving the library, it may be helpful to have some rules making books valuable in your game. The easiest way is to assign books monetary value – books were not common in the middle ages. A typical book on a random subject will be worth d10 gp to an interested dealer. The most common sort of magical books will be worth d10 x 10gp. A possibly more interesting option is to allow mechanical advantages to PCs who own or who have read certain books – see page 41. The most interesting and most difficult option is for the GM to devise specific pieces of campaign information to be hidden in specific "unusual-looking" books that a PC can find in certain libraries after a thorough search or successful check. More optional rules for libraries are included on page 41.

This location is designed to pose a challenge to PCs of levels 4 – 7 with few, if any, magic items. If your PCs possess an unusual number of magic items, or if those items are unusually powerful, you may wish to increase the levels of Zorlac and his minions. However, during playtests, the single most important factor for determining how difficult this scenario was turned out to be how clever, aggressive, and coordinated the NPCs were. If they coordinate their attacks and use the most deadly tactics available, the scenario could pose a challenge to any group.

If you lack faith in your players (or if they just hate puzzles), feel free to add extra clues to finding the secret doors.

The domestic half of Zorlac's home is strangely laid out – you have to walk through the bedroom to reach the kitchen. Smart players – or one's whose PCs are experienced in building or architecture – may realize that this is because secret chambers have been built where ordinary parts of a home once were in order to house Zorlac's ever-expanding collection.

Moving Around the Library (Map on the following page)

The secret doors leading to the exterior of the building can be discovered from outside by careful examination (a standard secret door check) provided whoever is checking can get to the appropriate part of the building. There are no stairways or walkways leading to them (Zorlac expects his thieves to be able to scale the gargoyles and crenellations of the library unaided.) From the inside, they look like regular doors.

The interior secret doors cannot be discovered by a standard secret door check. Each has a special mechanism that will simultaneously reveal and open it – explained in the room description. Secret doors leading to stairwells are obvious on the side facing the stairwell. In the libraries, the book cases move and slide to reveal the door. The triggers reset after use.

The ordinary doors leading outside and to the open – air bridges are all locked.

The libraries each consist of a single cylindrical room approximately 60 feet tall.

If the PCs enter secretly while he's home, Zorlac will begin in a random room (roll d20, no chance of being in the entrance hall) if the PCs enter surreptitiously. He will notice any loud noise in any nearby room.

Each library contains: a desk, a carpet, 3 comfortable chairs, 12 lanterns and a 57 foot ladder. The desk has an inkwell, quill pen, and various papers containing librarian's notes. Furnishings specific to each library are noted on the map key. The walls are lined up to their ceilings with (74 + d20) x 1000 books on shelves. The average book weighs d4 lbs.

When PCs enter a library roll d4:

1. Librarian is in the library
2. Librarian out
3. Librarian will return in d4 rounds
4. Librarian will return in d4 minutes

If the PCs are looking for a secret door, it helps to keep careful track of how much in-game time this takes.

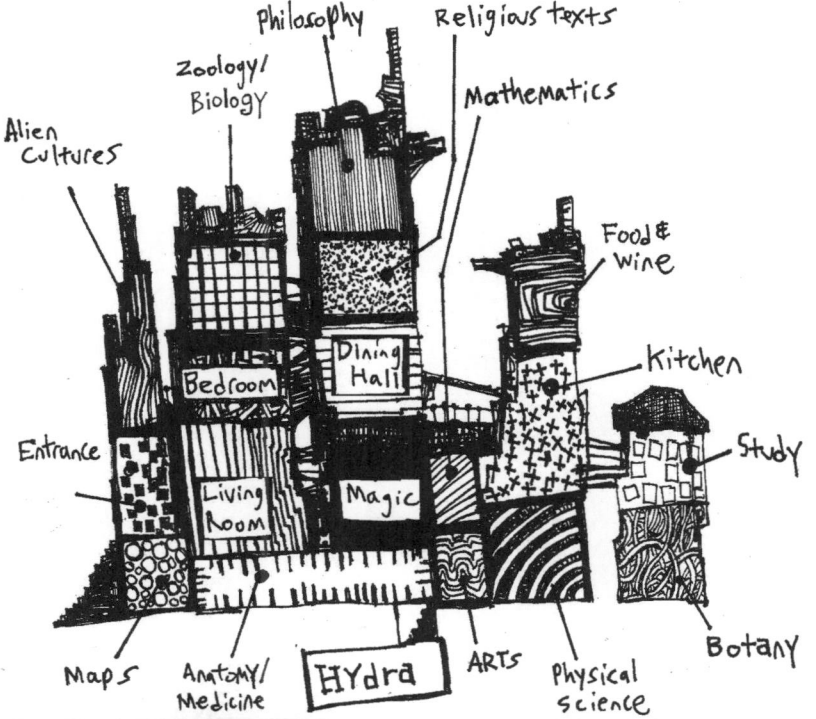

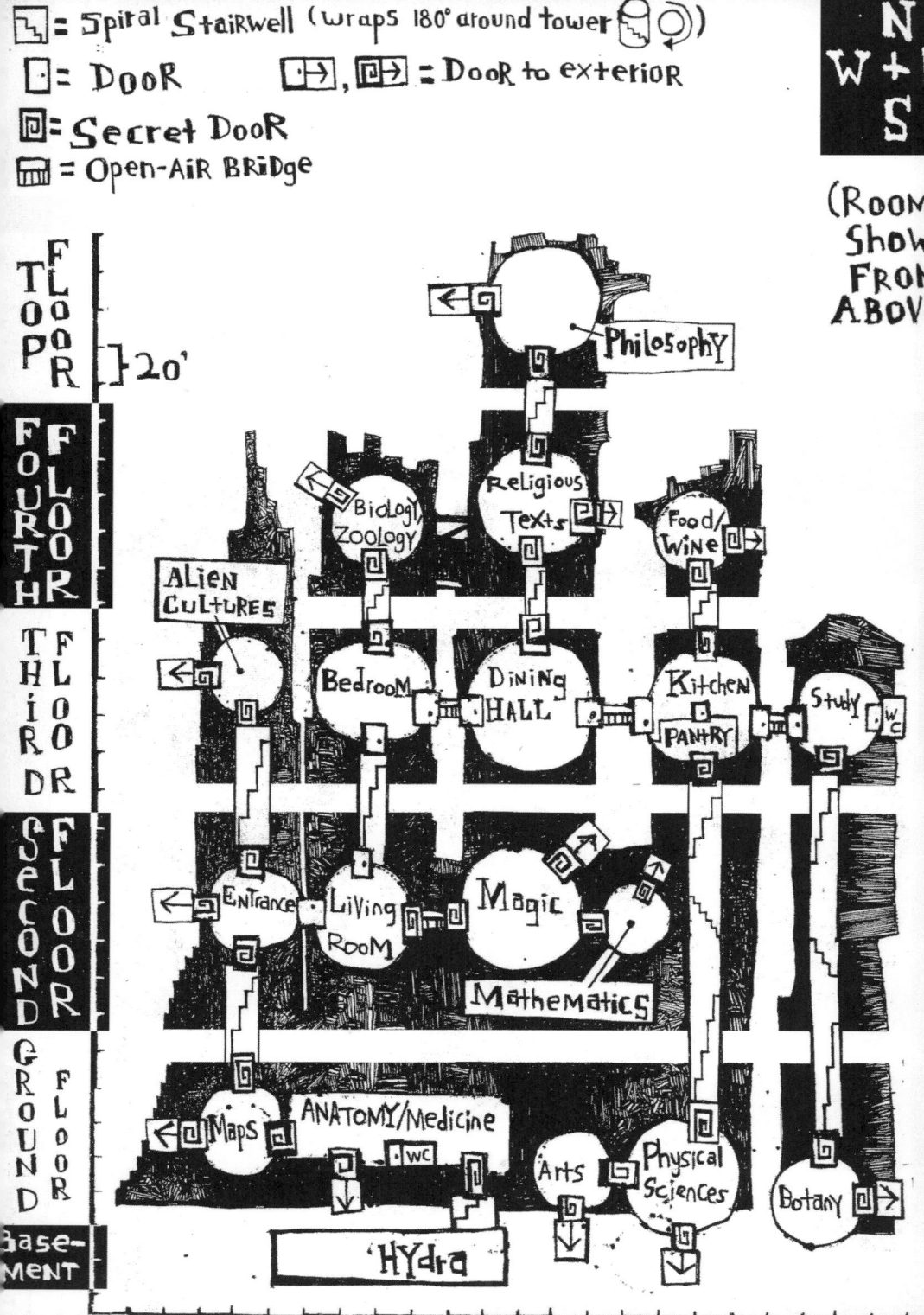

Alien Cultures Library
Works originally written in foreign languages and works the current Alien Cultures librarian translated. Various half-translated works lie about and there's a life-sized marble statue of a man with a missing head.

South Door Trigger Resting a head (severed or otherwise) where the statue's missing head is.

Biology/Zoology Library
On desk: box of preserved butterflies, stuffed lizard with one eye, fossil of a large claw, and a so-called "mermaid's purse" – a kind of shark egg.

South door trigger Mermaid's purse is false and opens like a wallet and contains a small socket-key. Placing it in the lizard's empty eye socket opens the door.

Maps Library
Atlases and works of geography. On wall: sea chart on parchment, on desk: a globe (in the world of Vornheim, this will be cube-shaped), a "bone globe" (a cube showing the tunnels beneath the earth – inaccurate), a continental map with each continent and body of water made with inlaid semiprecious stones – topaz, lapis, etc., with 1 continent and 1 lake missing. In desk drawer: package full of stale cookies/biscuits. On floor: crumbs.

East door trigger Biting a cookie into the shape of the missing continent and placing it where the continent should be.

North door trigger Biting a cookie into the shape of the missing lake and placing it where the lake should be.

Anatomy/Medicine Library
One of the desks' drawers is unpickably locked. On desk: small human skeleton in clay, preserved brain in a jar and 4 vials: yellow liquid, blue liquid, blue powder, green powder.

West door trigger Brain has a seam – opening it reveals a key fitting the desk's locked drawer. Turning the key in the lock opens the door.

East door is findable by an ordinary "secret door" check, but is locked. The key in the brain fits this door, as do keys the hydra tenders carry.

Magic Library
Spellbooks and theoretical works. On wall: diagrams of the planes of existence, diagram of the 16 elements and a copper model of the spheres of existence.

East and West door triggers Small brass switch underneath desk. Turning it east opens the west door and vice versa.

Arts Library
Works of literature, surveys of the arts, and technical manuals. On walls: 4 paintings (enamel on wood) depicting multifigure scenes with various courtiers and kings, the right-center scene depicts a cat.

East door trigger The figures' heads are painted on small free – spinning disks set into the paintings so they can be made to spin around on the surface of the painting. Turning all the heads toward the cat opens the door.

Physical Sciences Library
Chemistry, physics, engineering, etc. On wall: diagram on the wall showing the construction of a battlement and a meteorological diagram. The entire floor is a star map – each star is in a small divot. The Grey Star, Orlock is in the dead center. In desk: croquet set with freestanding hoops.

North door trigger Placing the red croquet ball in the divot marking the position of Orlock.

West door trigger Placing the blue ball in the position of Orlock.

Botany Library
Pots here contain: Blue-tendrilled Dydrangea, Flecked Blackfruit, Taloned Orchid. Also: a glass terrarium full of pink spherical slime mold.

North door trigger One of the chairs has a switch underneath the cushion.

Food/Wine Library
Cookbooks and surveys of cuisine. On walls: 4 still life paintings – fruit bowl with peaches, grapes and a plum, lobster feast, wine and bread.

South door trigger Plum is painted on a free-spinning disk, turning it 180 reveals the door.

Mathematics Library
There is an abacus made of glass, one of ivory and one of volcanic stone.

The West door is poorly constructed and a standard check for secret doors will reveal an irregularity in the bookcases. It can be pried open. Sliding the top stone on the ivory abacus back and forth 12 times will also activate the door.

Religion Library
Sacred texts and studies of religion. Marble statuettes of Vorn, Tittivilla and Parassik, the Night Serpent.

North door trigger Parassik's head swivels – turning it toward Tittivilla activates the door.

South door trigger Tittivilla's right breast swivels – turning it toward Parassik activates the door.

Philosophy Library
Philosophy and the humanities – including politics, law, military history, etc. Marble portrait busts of philosophers: Zorreal the Interpreter, Scurrilous Korp, Naxinoggol and Proscorpius.

South door trigger Reaching into Scurrilous Korp's mouth reveals a switch that opens the door.

Hydra Room
Contains knives, oven, poker for burning stumps of hydra heads, partial manuscripts and hydra. It wears enchanted shackles which restrain it during the day and sedate it at night. Hydra cannot be moved from the room unless the shackles are removed. There are enough manacles for each foot and as many as 14 necks. Without a neck manacle, a head is free to attack. Hydra tenders arrive at dusk and work until dawn – hydra is unattended during the daytime.

The Bedroom, Dining Hall, Kitchen, Pantry, Study, WCs and Entrance Hall
are opulent but unremarkable. The secret doors in these rooms can be found via careful examination of the walls or standard secret door checks. The furnishings in any one room are worth a total of d10 x 100 gp per room, but any dealer in Vornheim will know where they came from.

Living Room
Contains The Oblong Rug.

Library of Zorlac

Oblong Rug

Seemingly ordinary black and white rug containing an intricate pattern. Anyone examining it carefully must make three consecutive Wisdom rolls. If any fail, the observer gains a permanent insanity. If they all succeed, the observer gains a point of Wisdom or a vital insight into the nature of a mystery of the campaign (GM's choice). Looking a second time results in gaining an insanity.

Looking a *third* time will unlock the rug's true and transcendent metaphysical secrets – which allow him or her some thoroughgoing grasp of some vast and bizarre phenomenon underlying the entire campaign, such as: Mount Vrothgeist is the shape it is because creatures from the stars sculpted it with energy from the sun. (No one will know if this "insight" is actual real campaign information or if it's just a delusion the PC now believes to be true.)

Continued examination of the rug after that will result in a rupture in space/time with catastrophically bizarre consequences, causing thorough and permanent alterations to the character and campaign. (GM should decide what these are, since s/he will likely have to deal with them for many sessions to come.)

Zorlac

Although not trained in magic, Zorlac has acquired a smattering of useful spells during his years of study. He can be treated as a 10th level wizard for most purposes. If the party seems dangerous, Zorlac may not engage immediately, preferring instead to send the nearest librarian or hydra tender against the PCs. In emergencies, he will give them any information they need to pursue the PCs (and have them slain immediately after the emergency is over), in truly desperate situations he may release the hydra, or release a demon from the Oblong Rug.

Level: 10   **Hit Points**: 23

Armor: None   **Intelligence**: 16

Attack: Knife (d4hp)

Standard Spells (once/day): *Duo Dimension* (flattens caster to 2 dimensions for 10 rounds), *Distance Distortion* (doubles or halves distance between caster and target, range effectively infinite, duration: 10 minutes) (Unlike the standard version of this spell, Zorlac does not need an earth elemental's aid to cast this spell), *Mirror Image*, (creates 1 – 4 illusory duplicates of caster for 20 rounds – they disappear when struck) *Forget* (everyone in 12' x 12' square except caster forgets the last round permanently).

New spells (once/week) (100 ft range) *Discharge*: Cause any caster to save vs. spell or discharge any spell he or she has in a manner of Zorlac's choosing. *Vile Hound*: Cause a small dog to appear inside a target's body, causing d12 damage per round until it is removed. *Summoning Ritual*: Can summon dividing demons from the Oblong Rug using drops of blood Zorlac has spilled from any enemy in the last hour. Demons will obey Zorlac for 24 hours, but afterward they will obey no-one, so Zorlac will only use this ritual in the most dire situations. He can summon a maximum of four. He may slay one of his servants if he is in a real jam.

Defense: If Zorlac's blood is spilled by a foe on the Oblong Rug, one Dividing Demon (under Zorlac's control for 24 hours) will appear, if he remains on the rug, one will appear per round until he moves or is moved.

Dividing Demon

Human sized, bent, gaunt and gibbering, leathery black skin, red eyes.

HD: 10   **Speed**: as human

AC: 2 or 18   **Intelligence**: 9

Attack: 2 Claws (d8hp) or..Demon's body splits in half, each able to function normally and possessing half the original number of hit points. The demon may then, in the same round, attack once or touch a target and thereby similarly split a foe. On any subsequent round a successful grapple (Strength 16) check allows a half-demon to meld his/her body with the target's and use all of their abilities. This state of affairs lasts until the demon – half of the hybrid is slain. Obviously the demon can attempt to merge with two foes simultaneously (or one twice). Each half-demon has 1 claw attack.

Defense: Immune to poison and fire. Takes half damage from non-magic weapons unless they are iron.

Note: This demon can only inhabit rooms with an even number of living creatures in them (including the demon itself, but not including plants, microbes, insects etc.). Otherwise, it will flee to the nearest room which fits its requirements. (If the demon slays a living creature it will usually have to move.) The demon cannot go outside and cannot be alone. If it is unable to find any room it can occupy it will scramble, panicked, from room to room until the situation changes.

Hydra
Body is twice elephant-sized, 5 – 14 heads.

HD: d10+4 **Speed**: human
(each hit die represents a head)
AC: 5 or 15 **Intelligence**: animal

Attack: 1 bite for d8hp per head per round.

Defense: Each time the hydra loses a head (4 hp), it grows two new ones unless fire is applied to the wound.

Hydra tenders
Gropius, Gavulous, and Screebe
These three elderly wizard-scholars are charged with pruning the hydra's heads at intervals and translating the scales into the common tongue. They carry keys to its shackles and the secret door in the anatomy/medicine library. They arrive at dusk and work until dawn – the hydra is unattended during the daytime.

Level: 5 **Hit Points**: 12

Armor: None *Intelligence*: 17

Attack: Wavy daggers (d4hp) (at – 1 to hit). Each can cast *Sleep*, *Confuse Languages*, *Web*, and *Darkness 15' Radius* once per day. In addition, Gropius can cast *Slow*, Gavulous can cast *Suggestion*, and Screebe can cast *Dispel Magic* once per day.

Librarians
The following details apply to all librarians:

Level 8 thieves with 8 – 48hp. Armor: leather with a system-appropriate bonus for having 17 dexterity. Intelligence: 14 + d4

Equipment: Poison, rope, grappling hook, torch, light crossbow, 2 daggers, short sword.

Special abilities: bonus to hit with missile weapons (17 dexterity) (in addition to the to hit bonus given for their class level in systems that use such bonuses), 60% chance of knowing the language of any literate people or species. GMs should give them abilities appropriate to thieves/rogues/specialists level in their system.

Tactics: They will listen at the doors before opening them. If they hear anyone but Zorlac in their library they will usually lie in wait near (usually above or below) the door with crossbow ready and follow anyone leaving who might have a book until he or she is vulnerable. The first shot will be poisoned. The librarians will use hit-and-run tactics thereafter.

Librarians will use the most sophisticated tactics the GM can think up, however remember that the magical oaths they take upon entering Zorlac's service prevent them from working together *unless outsiders actually enter one of the libraries.*

Not all of the librarians are entirely loyal to Zorlac, but they will all shoot first and ask questions later.

Library of Zorlac

Stats and Details

Alien Cultures Librarian (Krask)

Speaks all languages in his section and has an 80% chance of being able to speak any other language that comes up. Has two words in a forgotten tongue tattooed on his right forearm, each is magical and acts as a scroll usable once (ever) each. One causes every target within a 30' radius to be unable to speak whatever single language is most common among them for 1 day (in most cases this will be "common"). No save.

The other allows Krask to vomit a small black toad into the air, which will land on a target within 15', the toad attacks (in the same round) as a 5 HD monster, if successful, the toad bites the target for d8 points of damage and the target will vomit up another toad (still in the same round) which will leap at the next available target (within 15') and attack in the same way and with the same consequences.

The process continues until one of the toad's attacks is unsuccessful. Toads dissolve into an inky black goo at the end of the round.

Krask despises Zorlac and will negotiate with the PCs if they offer him something of value, and only if they can convince him they'll be successful.

Biology/Zoology Librarian (Brigitte)

Expert on animals and monsters – will know the capabilities of any pets, summoned animals, or other beasts she is faced with. She has a white cat of an unusual breed named Moon that lives in the library. Moon's statistics:

HD: 3 **Speed**: 1.25x human
AC: 7 or 13 (Dex) **Intelligence**: animal (obeys Brigitte's commands)

Attack: Touch (d8+7 hp of electrical damage). In addition, attacking Moon or touching him with bare skin or any conductive material will cause similar damage.

Maps/Geo Librarian (Eero Vrollgatt)

White elf from Nornrik. Eeero knows Vornheim inside and out. If he can be made or forced to cooperate he may be able to reveal useful information about the location of much that is obscure and hidden in the city.

Anatomy/Med Librarian (Zeo Voreos)

Knowledge of anatomy gives him a +1 to damage against all humanoid creatures. An expert in the non-magical healing arts and, to the degree that such arts are effective in your version of the game, he can employ them. If attacked near his desk, he will grab a vial off the table, claim it contains a virulent and fast-acting airborne flesh-eating bacteria capable of eating away an adult's internal organs in seconds and threaten to throw it at the PCs if they do not leave at once. He is lying.

Magic Librarian (Corsica Nyne)

The magic library is so dangerous that Zorlac trusts no-one else with the knowledge contained therein – Zorlac himself is the closest thing the magic library has to a true librarian. Nyne is merely an assistant and book-thief, and has only an apprentice understanding of the works held therein.

She can cast *Invisibilty*, *Spider Climb*, and *Sleep* as a 3rd level wizard and will use them to ambush intruders.

Arts Librarian (Maarten Tull)

The smartest and most dissatisfied of the librarians. Knows where all of the hidden doors are. He fears Zorlac, however, and requires a great deal of persuading to take any action against him. Fond of liquor, women and poetry.

Physical Sciences Librarian (Olivia Vrak)

Vrak carries 3 vials of acid at all times for personal protection. On a successful hit, the acid causes 2 – 12hp of damage, on a miss *that would have hit discounting the victim's armor* the acid will eat a hole in the targets armor, worsening the target's AC by 2.

Botany Librarian (Nariya Remora)

During her studies, Remora has slowly built up an immunity to the particular form of plant-based neuromuscular poison she uses on her victims – consequently she doesn't fear casual contact with it and keeps *all her weapons and crossbow bolts coated in poison at all times*. If she is stabbed or hit with a blade contaminated with her own poison her save will be at +5.

Food/Wine Librarian (Lorb Doubloon)

Clever and insatiable gourmand. Doubloon has discovered the secret door leading to the kitchen and pantry, which he discreetly raids from time to time. Can occasionally be persuaded to trade information for exotic recipes, rare ingredients or fine food and drink.

Mathematics Librarian (Zoth Cataphract)

Unbeknownst to Zorlac, Cataphract's researches into extradimensional geometries have brought him into contact with things best left unknown. The frenzied prose in the notebook he carries at all times will make this clear to anyone who reads it. Cataphract is possessed by a demon named **Vortullax** which will manifest itself through Cataphract's body if he is captured or reduced to less than 5hp. When this occurs, his eyes become hollow, his skin shrivels and he begins to laugh maniacally...

HD: 8 **Speed**: as human
AC: 2 or 18 **Intelligence**: 13

Attack: Remove its head and throw it up to 30' to deliver a fanged bite for 2 – 12hp. If this bite connects the head will attempt to suck the victim's bones out through its skin – Constitution check or victim loses the bones in:

1-2	Upper Right Arm
3	Lower Right Arm
4-5	Upper Left Arm
6	Lower Left Arm
7-8	Left Side Ribs
9-10	Right Side Ribs
11-12	Upper Left Leg
13-14	Lower Left Leg
15-16	Upper Right Leg
17-18	Lower Right Leg
19	Pelvis
20	Skull

This will cause 2 – 12 additional points of damage or, in the case of the skull, kill the target.

Defense: Immune to poison and flame. Warps space around him such that no attack aimed at him will connect. (This effect will be visible to the attacker as a distortion of his/her field of vision). The only way to strike Vortullax is to purposefully aim the attack away from Vortullax and succeed in an ordinary to hit roll (prolonged study of Cataphract's diary and a successful Intelligence check will reveal this). A miss has a 50% chance of hitting any other creature in the area. Magic attacks which require no movement of material through space (such as "power word" spells) work normally unless they are cast by a caster with less than 8 levels, in which case they have a 50% chance of having bizarre and unpredictable effects.

Religion Librarian (Azima Ozaloth)

Carries a small black stone the size of a marble which makes its owner invisible to the gods – thus no cleric spells of any kind can affect her for good or ill. The stone does not radiate magic nor does it appear remarkable in any way under any form of scrutiny.

Philosophy Librarian (Maxilla Sorrn)

Unbeknownst to Zorlac, the employee he knows as Maxilla Sorrn is actually a pair of identical twins – Maxilla and Auxilla. Usually one will arrive at the library while the other waits until her sister is sure Zorlac isn't there, then they will spend the rest of the day or night working together. Only Maxilla took the oath, so Auxilla can see the other librarians – occasionally the sisters will use this knowledge to spy on or steal from the other librarians.

Player Handout

Player Commentaries

Player Commentaries

Here's a look at what Vornheim is like from the other side of the table, from the group who's spent the most time there...

Connie (C) and Frankie (F) play thieves/rogues/specialists, Mandy Morbid (MM) plays a cleric of Vorn, Kimberly Kane (KK) plays a barbarian, Satine Phoenix (SP) played a thief that died, then played a wizard/bard that died, and now has a monk.

On the Church of Vorn (pg 6)

MM: My impression is that it is nearsighted and corrupt, though powerful – and useful at times. There's a lot of people pretending like they don't know what the fuck is going on when they probably do and a lot of nuns and church people who actually don't know what's going on who are being used by a few powerful people in the system.

I've gone on dangerous missions for them in good faith that turn out to be detrimental to various populations' well being. But I like the Church's mix of, say, old school Catholic fanaticism and more occult, creepy, mysterious things, so it's fun to roleplay – it gives me a wide range of ways to behave that I can justify by saying "Well I'm a cleric of Vorn."

On The Wyvern of the Well (pg 8)

F: I thought I could charm the Wyvern, then I thought it was gonna double-cross me because it was so mysterious and powerful and I had to give it money... and I have anxiety.

C: Frankie really wanted the Wyvern to like her, I don't know why. I was happy that I got her to do all the asking and answering so I could save my question. When we heard that the Wyvern likes gold our first thought was we should probably try to rob the Wyvern but at that point we didn't know how big it was. It's weird, the Wyvern's price was so steep it pretty much forced us into crime.

On The Chain (pg 8)

C: The humunculus was disgusting – it really made me uneasy and unhappy and disturbed and displeased and seemed really hard to kill... no-one likes things that are hard to kill. I found the sight of it unsettling. I didn't like that it was fast and ugly and deadly and it could crawl in your eye or nose, no one likes things to crawl in their eye or nose.

On Eshrigel the Medusa (pg 11)

KK: Killing the ghoul with the medusa's daughter's head was one of my most ingenious killing sprees.

SP: We actually spent way more time worrying about the medusa than fighting her. This is the magic of RPGs. This is the magic of an adventure. The reality is that the villain is just an idea with stats, but the fun part is that we can scare ourselves and make the idea of the villain bigger and more exciting than it really is; over-villainizing the villain. Thinking of all the possible ways she could attack us, sneak up on us, etc. makes the game more exciting and gives us a reason to be more creative and clever. The more intensely we imagine her the more intensely we imagine defending ourselves. Collectively we all knew the myth of Medusa and this previous knowledge got us excited and thinking of ways to face her and ultimately defeat her so we could use her head as a weapon.

C: I don't think i was really concerned. I just decided I wasn't gonna look at her. I think I... didn't I strap a mirror to my forehead or something? Yeah. I figured then she'll turn herself to stone, then she'll know how it feels.

On The Library of Zorlac (pg 24)

MM: I was in the library very briefly, the librarian we met was funny, he was charming. I offered to sell him some books, my sister got a job as a maid and went snooping around, we were attacked by a librarian and then some horrible abomination attacked and I lost a leg but escaped with my life. I don't know if the fire that got started damaged the actual library. I also don't know what the abomination being let loose in the streets in the middle of the day did to Zorlac's reputation. Given the chance, I'd definitely go back – it is a castle full of books.

On Random Tables (pg 44)

KK: I think the charts are made up of 1 – 20 or 1 – 100 things and I think one of all of these is possibly a good thing and the rest are bad, and you're trying to kill us.

ZS: How come you're not dead?

KK: 'Cause I elude you.

ZS: Is it fair to say they fill you with dread?
KK: Yes. Just once I'd like to roll on a table and get a horse.

On Random NPCs (pg 50)

KK: Those random guys are fun, Mandy seems to get good info, I always end up having sex with them to get information and then there isn't any information. Like I'll have sex with the vet to have drugs and there's no drugs. Shopkeepers turn me on, I guess, I like their accents.

On Hairdressers in Vornheim (pg 50)

F: If I was a hairdresser in Vornheim I would probably shave all of their heads except the top so they could have a ponytail coming from the top of their head. If a duchess came in and wanted a special haircut for a ball then I wouldn't cut it, I would dye it. I would braid it and make it crazy and big and people would be like "What the fuck, my hair's so crazy, nobody else could have this hair because I'm that important!"

On Taverns (pg 62)

KK: They're always fun because I imagine the same like old western spaghetti movie, even though it's not that – dancing girls and criminals and an upstairs with rooms and madness. I love the taverns.

C: When I went out in Vornheim I had too much too drink. I had a good time, but I had so much to drink that I probably would've had a good time anywhere.

SP: Surviving in Vornheim. Rule #1, 3, 32 & 59: Do not get drunk, tipsy, trip on drugs, or alter your perception in any way. You could be assaulted at any time by anything. Also, avoid speaking to anyone if you do find yourself drunk, tipsy, tripping on drugs or altering your perception in any way.

C: Hey, that's the game, you always get attacked, might as well have fun.

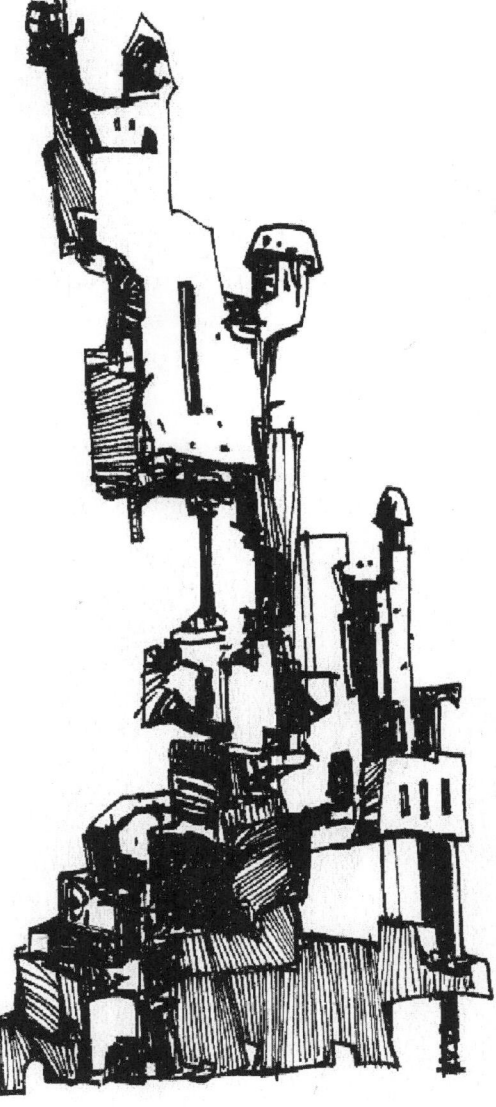

Typical Tower

- Wealthy Home
- Cistern
- Furnace (Heats snow creating water)
- Bridge
- Watchtower
- Book-Binder
- Bridge
- Wealthy Home
- Homes
- Fortuneteller
- Bridge
- Hat Shop
- Inn
- Cheesemaker
- Bridge
- Law Office
- Butcher
- Tavern
- Locksmith

Navigation Shortcuts for Busy GMs

Vornheim is big, big enough to be mysterious and noiry and, in that way, bigger than any real medieval city. This is why the large map included with this book only shows "inner" Vornheim – the city sprawls shapelessly in every direction as far as you like. The only way the players can develop a clear understanding of its overall geography is by playing. Handily, this also means there aren't a lot of facts for the GM to remember. There's a palace, a cathedral and a well in the center of town, there's a wall around that center, and the rest is up to you. This city is meant to feel more like a dungeon than a vacation spot in a tour book – it's an amorphous dark space through which the characters grope and carve their way over the course of their adventures. The First Rule is: once a place is explored, it's fixed on the map. Until then, though, anything the GM hasn't written down is up for grabs.

Neighborhoods

Rather than drawing a map and nailing down the exact shape of the city, you can make a quick neighborhood map like this one by writing out numbers 1 through 10 (or 12, or 20) in different colored markers more or less randomly. For this example, we'll say Vornheim has 10 neighborhoods, which is about a third as many as LA or Manhattan but it's about twice as many as Fritz Lieber appeared to need to write all of his famous Lankhmar stories.

The map doesn't show the actual shape of the city, just where neighborhoods are relative to each other and where the major streets and bridges are (Vornheim has building-to-building bridges everywhere – but for these rules, the bridges aren't necessary). For example, the fastest route from neighborhood ten to neighborhood four is via neighborhoods five or six, though you could go 10 – 9 – 2 – 1 – 4 if, for example, there was a giant lizard eating neighborhoods 5 and 6.

The major thoroughfares roughly match all the lines in the words spelling out the numbers in the neighborhood map. i.e. to get from neighborhood ten to neighborhood seven the PCs need to walk across a big "x" shaped intersection – and if they flew in a balloon over neighborhood six you'd see that the major streets spelled out the word "six". Remember that this is just the default street map for if a neighborhood is improvised during play. You always have the option of mapping more realistic streets in any part of town, as long as the PCs haven't been through it yet. Plus, if you count the bridges, there's several "layers" of connecting streets.

How are these neighborhoods different? Which is rich and which is poor, which are full of shops and which full of homes? In the author's experience, creating a game supplement which goes into too much detail on this merely forces the GM to memorize names and distinctions invented by someone else before feeling comfortable enough with the setting to use it. Yes, Vorheim has neighborhoods – rich ones, poor ones, commercial ones and residential ones and ones of ill fame and ones full of immigrants, but so does every other large city. Decide before a session, figure out which neighborhood is which in the course of the game, or decide for each neighborhood randomly: roll d4 for wealth level (2 and 3 are medium), roll on the random building table (on the Inside Back Cover) to see what the most prominent landmark is, roll again on the random building table to see what kind of business is most characteristic of the area, roll d20 to see what percentage of the population is nonhuman, and roll on the encounter table to see what will happen next time the PCs visit it at night.

Kinds of Buildings

For the purposes of these rules, there are only two kinds of buildings: the kind that are all over the place (common buildings) and the kind you can count (landmark buildings). We'll deal with landmark buildings first. Vornheim has 1 Arena, 1 Barracks, 2 Prisons, 3 Major theaters, 1 Spymaster's secret headquarters,

Urbancrawl Rules

1 major cathedral, 5 competing cathedrals, and 1 Palace.

If, in the middle of an adventure, the PCs suddenly need to know where one of these things is and it's not already on the map, or find some other unique place (a certain duke's home, for instance), roll a d10.

That's what neighborhood it's in. Or, if you prefer, you can simply drop any die onto the Central Vornheim map – wherever the die lands, that's where it is.

Common buildings, on the other hand, are everywhere. Assume every neighborhood contains at least one of the kinds of buildings listed in the random Building table (Inside Back Cover). (This is probably unrealistic. Is there necessarily a cheesemaker in every neighborhood in a medieval city? No. But in a pinch, it'll do.)

Moving Vs. Crawling

In a dungeon or wilderness adventure everything is hard – navigating, finding food, getting a decent night's sleep, etc. – and so everything is part of the adventure. Adventuring in a city is fundamentally different from adventuring in a dungeon or wilderness because cities are actually meant for habitation. In most cities, many things will be easy and therefore not part of the adventure and the GM has to do a great deal of deciding when to "zoom in" and deal with the situations in more detail. For this reason we're going to create a distinction between simply "moving" through the city and "crawling" through it.

The relationship of 'crawling' to 'moving' is like the relationship of 'escaping' to merely 'leaving'. 'Crawling' only occurs when passage through the city is difficult or mysterious for some reason and so, therefore, the choice of route and means of locomotion between points is important. 'Crawling' occurs when:

- The PCs are being chased.
- The PCs are in a hurry.
- A large number of elements in the city are actively hostile to the PCs (such as during an invasion or plague of madness).
- The PCs are systematically searching a small area of the city for something.
- The PCs are trying to avoid running into someone or something.
- It's night.
- The city is transformed in some way such that it ceases to function like a city (post-nuclear bomb, etc.).
- The PCs don't really know where they're going.
- There's urgency attached to the PC's decisions about how to proceed for any reason.

Merely 'moving' is simple. The PCs say where they're going and the GM can describe the journey (keeping in mind that the more s/he describes, the more things the PCs have the option of interacting with) or simply shift the scene to the destination. Things get more complicated if the PCs are crawling:

Crawling From Neighborhood to Neighborhood

If the PCs are crawling toward a destination that's in another neighborhood, roll one random encounter (pg 54) for each neighborhood boundary they cross.

If the PCs don't know where they're going, they can ask a random stranger for directions. Make a Reaction Roll or try to roll under Charisma on a d20. Success means they get where they're going. If they fail, the stranger isn't charmed enough to give conscientious directions. Consult the Directions table on page 53.

Crawling Within A Neighborhood

When PCs are crawling in the same neighborhood as whatever they're looking for and the neighborhood isn't mapped yet, the GM rolls 2d10 on a piece of paper. Look where the dice land: the positions of the two dice represent the relative positions of the PCs and their destination. (If the PCs entered the neighborhood from the south, the southmost die is the PCs' position, from the north, the northmost is the PCs position, etc.). Now look at what's on the PC's die: The streets between the PC and his/her objective are shaped like whatever number comes up on the die. For example, if the PC comes into the neighborhood from the north and the GM rolls a "1" on the northmost die then the map to wherever the PC is going to looks like this:

If the PCs take a wrong turn and unwittingly run off the edge of the "1" into an unknown zone, simply roll a d10 again for the location of the next place and the layout of the streets they just ran onto. Over time, once the PCs have been a few places in a neighborhood, the "known streets" of the neighborhood might look like this...:

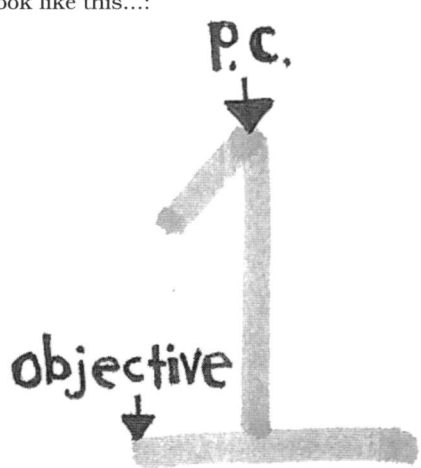

...and the GM can flesh out the neighborhood at will and throw in "decoy" streets to disguise the scheme from the players (they won't be able to see the layout from the PC's eye view anyway) – it's easy, numbers are just straight lines and circles.

That's the same neighborhood after 5 seconds of extra streets. All this is more complicated if you take into account the bridges, but for the sake of a single day's adventure this will work fine. If a PC is on a bridge and gets knocked off to a lower "level" and doesn't climb back up, just start the process all over again on the lower city level.

This method can also be used if the PC's aren't "crawling" but merely want to map the neighborhood they're in for future reference. Remember, the streets aren't necessarily shaped like numbers – it's just that the segment of their journey that lies between them and their goal is.

Floorplan Shortcut

Unlike dungeons and most adventure locations you might've prepared in advance, the floorplans of random homes and businesses aren't terribly complex or interesting (and they don't usually need to be). A quick survey of real floorplans and ones in most RPG products will confirm they generally consist of a number of adjacent rectangles placed more – or – less at random. If the PCs enter an unmapped building, roll a d4 on a piece of paper, then draw straight lines outward from the d4 to the edge of the paper like so:

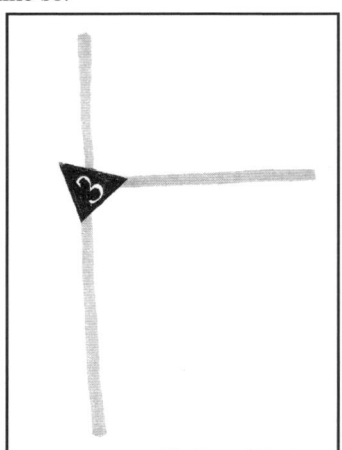

Draw a number of lines equal to the number rolled. To make a more complex plan, simply roll more dice and draw more lines.

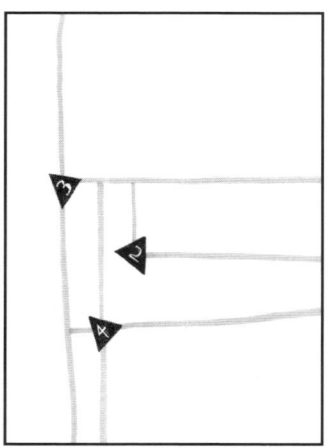

Unless it's a special building (secret lair, etc.), assume there are doors between every room and every adjacent room. For nonrectangular buildings, simply draw a quick outline of the building before tossing the dice.

Another method is to roll a standard d6 with "pips": the layout of rooms on a given floor will roughly match the layout of the dots, i.e.:

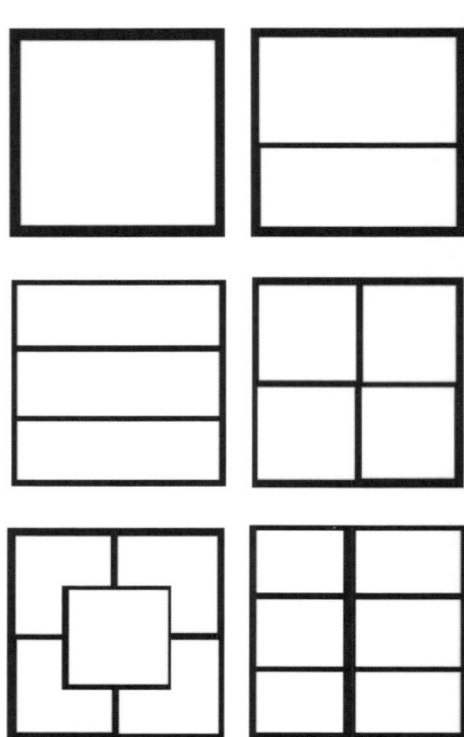

If it becomes relevant, roll 2d6 to determine number of floors (in Vornheim, anyway, for a more realistic city, roll a smaller die). Each floor can be laid out the same or differently, depending on how frantic the pace of the game is. For major buildings, just roll more dice and put the layouts next to each other.

The Law

Some say the system of overlapping and alternating legal processes in Vornheim is cunningly designed so that habitual criminals won't be able to learn to "game the system", some say they compose a thicket of unpruned barbaric traditions that've outlived their usefulness and some say the judges of Vornheim are simply insane.

At any rate, the law itself varies only slightly within Vornheim (rules regarding public drunkenness, openly carrying arms, and sumptuary laws preventing commoners from wearing clothes above their station being the laws most subject to change) but the trial processes for prosecuting breaches of law differ wildly from neighborhood to neighborhood and even from day to day (local churches, for instance, have legal jurisdiction during feast days). From the point of view of any but legal professionals, the jurisdiction at any given moment is essentially random (roll on the Legal Situation Table – page 59 – to determine what kind of trial will occur if a PC is arrested). A lawyer can be rented for d4 gp + (d20 per point of Charisma, Intelligence or Wisdom over 12) per day. PCs who have a lawyer as a contact may get better rates. Most of the trial-by-jury systems allow the accused's friends (the other PCs) to aid in the defense.

Some or even most of the legal situations presented on the table may strike many GMs as ludicrous, but remember 3 things: (1) Many of these are based on actual medieval trial rules, the theory being that god favors the innocent in chance situations (2) It is almost impossible for PCs to have adventures in a city without breaking the law, therefore, in order to have a meaningful city-based game that feels different from a dungeon or wilderness game, arrest – or at least the threat thereof – should be a part of the game and in order to have a fun game the arrest process should lead to something unexpected and interesting rather than just meaning the game grinds to a halt and (3) you can always ignore these rules if you feel like it.

Once a result has been used the GM may cross it out and write his or her own, or leave the result in the mix.

Contacts

Rather than using "gather information", "streetwise" checks, or other similar mechanics, GMs and players can use these rules to add more detail to the investigative situation, as in a crime novel or film. Assume PCs who are city natives or who have spent more than a month living more-or-less normally (i.e. not tied up in a sack somewhere) in the city know a number of random city denizens equal to 1 + 1 per Charisma point over 15. Roll these contacts as random NPCs. In addition, PCs gain an extra contact every time they level up while in the city.

In addition, Thieves/Rogues/Specialists or other "streetwise" classes start off with 1 extra contact. This all may seem rather stingy but keep in mind that most PC parties contain 3 – 7 members and that PCs naturally acquire contacts with no help from the rules during many adventures.

The Contacts table on page 52 can be used when a contact (or any other citizen the PCs have managed to stay on good terms with) is asked about any subject that is not desperately obscure, but that they still would not be expected to know anything about. It helps if the players know the roll is random – that way they'll know that asking around always has a chance of being useful independent of what the GM or adventure intends. This way, contacts become another weapon in the arsenal rather than a tool of a pre-planned plot, and the PCs know it.

Optional Rules for Chases

If two parties moving ostensibly at the same speed are in a chase situation, both roll d10 and add their Dexterity (if running across uneven or obstacle – laden ground like a marketplace or a building) or Strength (if over open, flat ground). Whoever rolls lowest loses a number of table top inches equal to the difference in the rolls or a number of feet equal to 6 x the number rolled. Do this every round until one party gives up or the parties meet. If both parties roll the same number at the same time, roll an encounter. If either party rolls a "1" at any time, then an obstacle – applecart, overweight vicar, etc. – has fallen in the way and the party must make additional rolls to avoid it.

Item Cost Shortcut

In wilderness and dungeon adventures, PCs spend most of any adventure isolated from anywhere they can buy equipment. In a city, PCs can buy new equipment almost whenever they want. Although it can be interesting to draw out shopping trips (see City Shopkeepers pg 52) Some GMs may find it helpful to have a shopping shortcut in order to move the adventure along faster.

Here's a rule of thumb using 5 categories called "Penny, Nickel, Dime, Quarter, Dollar":

- **Penny** items include any item a commoner might buy in an average day. This system assumes all the items an ordinary person buys in a typical day add up to one gp (or whatever the base unit of currency in your campaign is). A humble meal or two, a needle, a "dose" or three of beer, a torch, etc. all cost less than a gp.
- **Nickel** items include basic adventure/camping gear: Rope, pole, spikes, lantern, etc. these things cost 5 gp per syllable ("lantern" is 2 syllables – 10 gp).
- **Dime** items are specialist items – anything that usually only a certain profession or class would use or something that an ordinary person might only buy once. Thieves tools, navigation tools, a bible, a marionette, a table or a chair. Dime items cost 10 x number of syllables in the name. So: a lute costs 10 gp, a cello would cost 20.
- **Quarter** items are luxury items. A string of pearls, fancy shoes, etc. 25 gp x number of syllables in the name. A "Rich old woman's clothes" would be 125 gp. (You'll notice women's clothes always cost 25 gp more than men's.)
- **Dollar** items are things which are lethal or highly dangerous all by themselves – drugs and dangerous animals included. 100 gp per syllable – poison and acid would be 200 gp per dose, a wardog or falcon would be 200 gp, gunpowder or a heavy warhorse would be 300 gp, etc.
- Weapons: Melee weapons cost gp = maximum normal damage. Missile weapons cost twice that.
- Armor: Armor is important, expensive, and doesn't lend itself to simplification. If PCs need new armor, it's probably best to look it up.
- Food animals (chickens, turkeys) cost gp equal to the number of days food they represent.

The syllable thing sounds silly but more syllables generally indicates the PC wants a more specific thing (i.e. not just "rope" but "silk rope" not just "a lantern" but "a hooded lantern"). If you ask for something general you're going to get the humblest item that qualifies – like if you ask for a "horse" you won't get a warhorse, and if you ask for a "warhorse" you won't get a heavy warhorse.

So, yeah, that's that. All kinds of things are unrealistically pricey or cheap when you do this, but remember, this is just for when you're trying to get things to move fast. If you have time to look up items, do it.

Optional Rules for Libraries

As mentioned earlier, books are more interesting if they allow players to do new things after they've read a book on that subject (and if the players know that's how it works). A simple mechanic is to allow a +1 or re-roll on questions about a subject if the PCs read a book about it.

Obviously if a PC actually has a book on, say, geometry, with them while trying to answer a question about geometry, the question becomes even easier. If the PC has a book and time to consult it, s/he should get a +2. (Keep in mind that books before movable type are heavy, valuable, and fragile. Though the idea of a book on geology being standard issue gear along with a torch and 10' pole is appealing.)

Another – even simpler – option is to allow the owner of a book on a given subject to answer a certain given number of questions on that subject before it becomes useless. A very useful book might be a "10-question book" and a relatively unimportant one might be a "2-question book".

However, not all books are equally valuable to all PCs. A book that gives a PC a bonus to a knowledge check on a subject has to be one that: (A) Contains information the PC doesn't already know, but (B) Is written at a level that the PC can understand. A book that teaches a barely-literate barbarian a little more about geometry than s/he already knew will be useless to a mathematician and vice versa.

Any single random book has a 1 in 20 chance of being helpful to a given PC. If a PC searches a large library assume s/he will find 1 useful book every 20 minutes. If the library is multilingual, add +1 for each language the PC knows. These numbers can also be modified if the library has a specific focus that makes a given PC more or less likely to find a useful work – an alchemy library, for instance, will be heavily slanted toward books only those with a high intelligence can understand. If a PC is consistently played as someone with an interest in (say) taxidermy and s/he is in a library devoted to taxidermy, a bonus should be given.

To find the subject of a random book, roll d100 on the Books table (p48). The list has been broken down by broad subject to make it easier to randomize if the PCs find themselves in a "focused" library.

GMs may wish to invent a few could-be-anything titles to have at the ready rather than simply saying the topic of the book. For example, after a roll, you could tell the player "You've found 'The Book of Beelbe' – it appears to be about insects" or "You got 'The Clutching Cow' – it's a poem about a cow that grabs people." The Tavern names table (pg 62) can double as a random fiction work name table.

Searching Libraries

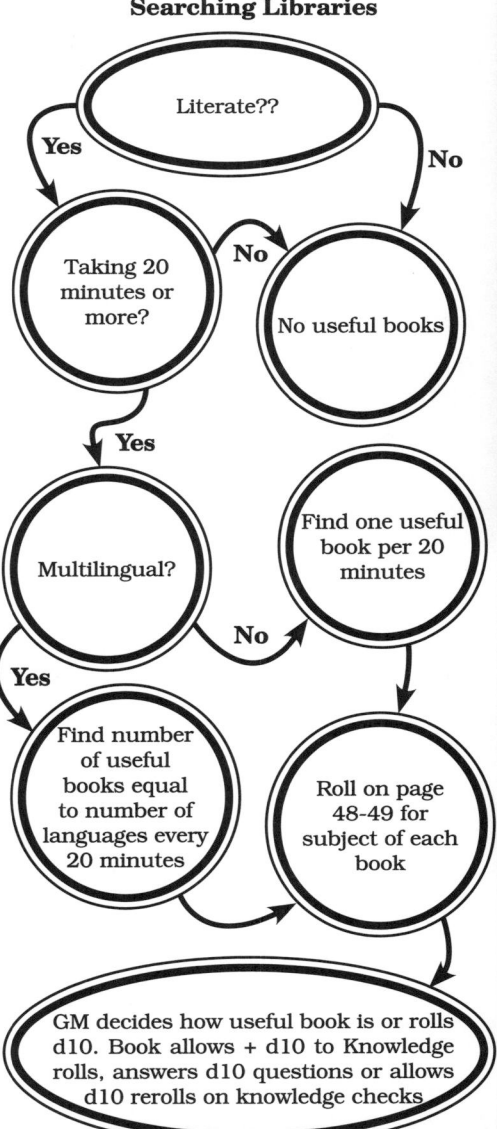

Some Notes on Open-Ended City Adventures

If a game is tightly plotted or is designed to last only one session, a city adventure is much like an adventure anywhere else. If the game is more of a "sandbox" and the PCs are free to roam as they will and choose their own goals, there are some important things to remember when GMing a city:

- In a wilderness or dungeon, the party's adventure during any given session is defined by where they are *geographically* – in a volcano, in the southwest corner of a maze, at the bottom of a pit, etc. In a city, this is less important, movement is freer, easier and more certain than in a dungeon and distances are shorter than in a wilderness. In a city, the party's adventure is defined by where they are in a *chain of consequences*. What's most important, after a session, is not figuring our where the PCs left off, but who they pissed off getting there. The next session's adventure can often be built from the consequences of what the PCs did during the last session.

- If the city becomes too dangerous for too little reward, PCs will just leave. The city must have rewards and details that interest the players if it is to become a re-usable location.

- Always give players as much information as you think they can handle at one time about things going on in the city. This allows them to make real choices about what to do and what resources to marshal, rather than just agreeing or not agreeing to investigate whatever the GM puts in front of them that day. A mass email could work for some groups, a large map with notes or a calendar pinned on the wall in the room where the game is played might work best for another.

Further Reading

Inspirations for Vornheim & Its World : Fritz Leiber (Lankhmar stories), M. John Harrison (Viriconium stories), Julio Cortazar (*Blow Up & Other Stories*, *Cronopios y Famas*), Jack Vance (Dying Earth stories), HP Lovecraft, Walt Simonson *Thor*, Poetic Edda, Prose Edda, John Gardner *Grendel*

Buildings David Macaulay *Castle*, Kristina Kruger *Monasteries & Monastic Orders*

Monsters www.rolang.com/archives/tag/medusa, JL Borges *Book of Imaginary Beings*

Libraries Anything about the Library of Alexandria, Borges *Collected Nonfictions*

Urbancrawl Ideas and Contacts Raymond Chandler, Dashiell Hammett, *The Big Sleep* (film)

GM Shortcuts http://recedingrules.blogspot.com/

Chases *The French Connection*, James Bond, *Face/Off* (films)

Schemes & Schemers *The Wire* (TV Show), *Fresh* (1994 film), Akira Kurosawa *Ran* (Film), Vladimir Nabokov, Michael Moorcock (*Elric* stories), William Shakespeare: *Macbeth* & *Hamlet*

The Law Lewis Carroll *Alice" Adventures In Wonderland*, *Through The Looking Glass*

People Terry Jones' *Medieval Lives* (TV show)

God's Chess

This is an extension of the ordinary rules of RPGs that can be used by players and GMs interested in exploring the political machinations among various factions within a city (or continent, or world, if the campaign is played out on that canvas). God's Chess is played *between* ordinary sessions of the game, and the results of God's Chess matches should be reflected by changes in the world of the ordinary game during the next session.

Step 1: Take a map of the city (or continent, or world) and grid it off into an 8-row, 8-column grid – like a chessboard.

Step 2: A player (one who likes to play chess) chooses a faction in the RPG whose interests are more-or-less aligned with his or her PC's. For example: a player playing Robin Hood might choose The Merry Men, and a player playing a loyal cleric of some god might choose that god's church. The GM chooses a rival faction (for example, the soldiers of Prince John, or a satanic cult).

Step 3: The GM and player play an ordinary game of chess – on the gridded map or on a normal chessboard.

Step 4: When the game is finished, the two players then note which pieces remain on the board and which square they occupy (with reference to the corresponding squares of territory on the gameworld map).

- A bishop in a given square means that chess player's faction has a cleric sympathetic to them in that area. For example, if the 'Merry Men' player has a bishop resting on the square corresponding to the northernmost neighborhood in the city, then maybe Friar Tuck lives in that neighborhood. His or her PC may be able to call on that cleric for aid in the next game.
- A rook in a given square means that chess player's faction controls a building in that area. For example, if the GM is representing a cult and has a rook in the southeastern neighborhood of the city, that means the cult controls a temple, orphanage, etc. in that part of town.
- A knight in a given square means that chess player's faction knows a sympathetic warrior or fighter in that area.
- A queen in a given square means that chess player's faction knows a sympathetic noble in that area.
- A pawn in a given square means that chess player's faction has an ordinary commoner sympathetic to them in that area.
- Kings mean nothing.

The power (and possibly number) of NPCs a surviving piece represents should be proportionate to the scale of the conflict in the RPG. If, for example, the chess game is played between two rival nations on a map representing a continent, then a remaining bishop might represent a whole city whose religious establishment is sympathetic to the player's country.

GMs wishing to make God's Chess a regular feature of their campaign might want to devise mechanisms whereby the PCs can gain an advantage in a given chess match due to their party's actions during the preceding game's session (for example, defeating an evil priest might allow the player to begin the chess game with the GM missing a bishop.)

Inventive GMs will find that most wargames, as well as games of territory-control such as *Citadels*, *Samurai*, and *Lyssan* can be adapted to a "God's Chess"-like schema. The main requirement is that the game be the kind which can end even if both (or all) players still have assets on the board.

Table Explanations

Table Explanations

These tables are not probability-based. They are designed to provide a variety of colorful and useful details when needed and to do so quickly, not to realistically simulate the workings of a believable world.

They won't help simulate the chances of things happening on any given day, they will help simulate the chances of things happening on an *interesting* day.

Sometimes tables can slow things down and this is bad. Sometimes, however, tables can slow things down and that's *good*. There are times when the GM saying, "Oh, wait, I have a *table* for that…" can create far more dramatic tension than any dragon or lizardman.

Here are some details on how and when to use the various tables in this section:

Aristocrats (p 46)

Roll once to select a fully-detailed NPC or roll once for each column to generate a unique aristocrat. The last column shows the relationship of the NPC to the next NPC and can be used to inveigle the PCs into complex conspiracies but can be ignored if the campaign isn't moving that way.

Note that gender-specific words (wife, husband, his, her) have been used, obviously these can be changed if a detail is being used for an NPC of a different gender.

City NPCs (p50)

This list is not meant to be an exhaustive list of medieval professions (there were a lot of them – someone who sells eggs was called an "eggler" – you want to make a d200 chart so there's room for an "eggler"? Someone who made scabbards was called a "vaginarius".) or demographically representative of the distribution of professions in Vornheim (more than 1% of Vornheimers are children, for example) but is merely meant as a tool for a busy GM to quickly create characters and situations with a reasonable level of variety and depth in mid-session until such time as s/he is able to sit down with the campaign materials and decide exactly where to add detail, and to give players a sense that a genuine and consistent world exists in all directions. Roll once and read across to quickly select an NPC or roll once for each column to create a unique character.

After details/notes have been used, cross them out and write your own. A blank in the second column indicates the NPC does not use a family name. If 'roll again' is indicated in the third column, re-roll for that column only.

Connections Between NPCs Diagram (p53)

Use this chart to create relationships among NPCs you've introduced. Write the NPC's names into the circles (pick or roll d4) and then roll to find his/her relationship to the others. Note that the central rectangle is used to show the relationship of NPC 1 to NPC 4 and the relationship of NPC 2 to NPC 3.

Encounters (p54)

In a dungeon or wilderness, almost any creature the PCs come across counts as an "encounter". A city, however, will be teeming with intriguing people and things that PCs can (and perhaps should) ignore on their way to wherever it is they're going. This table, therefore, is slanted toward ***unavoidable*** encounters – or at least ones which will have consequences if ignored.

The GM is of course free to devise less intrusive encounters – interesting objects left out on the street, NPCs acting bizarrely but minding their own business, etc. – but the results on this table are specifically designed to activate the city as an adventure location, and to ensure that players take the prospect of moving across it seriously. GMs just wanting to know who happens to be around at any given moment, can simply roll on the City NPCs table (pg 50).

Note also that exotic monsters such as vampires and werewolves are largely excluded from this list – encounters with such creatures tend to be more interesting and memorable if they're rare and carefully thought out by the GM in advance rather than having these unsettling creatures just be a regular hazard of city life. Also – it's hard to base a campaign in a city if it's so dangerous that any smart PC would want to leave immediately.

After a result has been used, cross it out and write your own, unless it is a marked with a *.

Fortunes (p56)

Nearly every known form of fortune-telling is practiced in Vornheim, from throwing runes to tarot cards to outlandish and brutal methods involving blood-stain analysis after human sacrifices.

Once a fortune is delivered to a PC, both GM and player make a note of it. Either one may announce that the fortune has come true any time the conditions implied by the premise of the fortune occur. For example: fortune #81 cannot come to pass until the player falls or is put to sleep during the ordinary conditions of the game and #99 can only happen at night, but #96 could occur in any inhabited area. Whether a PC in a lava prison in a dimension of fire demons could trigger #88 and suddenly a bearded woman would appear at the bars of the cell is a GM's call. Once the GM or player announces a fortune is being used it happens and it cannot be triggered again. Players may wish to trigger bad fortunes early, before the GM does it in more dangerous circumstances.

If a prediction has more than one part (such as #74), the parts do not necessarily have to both happen immediately and either party may trigger any part of it, so long as the time order (if any) implied in the prediction is respected.

More powerful forms of divination tend to be more dangerous and produce more than one fortune.

After a result has been used, cross it out and write your own.

"I Search the Body" (p58)

Assume every NPC is carrying d6 gp, house keys, a knife, tools necessary for their work (if applicable), and then roll on this table. Once a result is rolled, cross it out and write your own, unless it is marked with a *.

Magic Effect (p60)

It can be useful to have a simple spell, curse, or spell-like effect handy if you're improvising and a wizard or magic trap is called for. Duration and range can be tailored to the situation as can the saving throw. These can be fleshed out into full spells by the GM later if the PCs find some way to replicate the effect. Once a result is rolled, the GM may choose to cross it out and write a new one.

Taverns and Games (p62)

Roll once and read across to generate a full tavern quickly or roll once for each column to make a unique location. Mechanics of games are left to the GM, as systems for resolving noncombat tasks vary widely. Only games specific to Vornheim are explained.

After a result has been used, a GM may choose to cross it out and write his or her own.

Aristocrats

Roll	Name	Title	Description
1-2	Leopold	Von Vorg	Pulls wings off exotic butterflies from distant lands
3-4	Bastet	Von Vorg	Drowns orphans in bathtub
5-6	Vollrath	Von Klaw	Create wax sculptures of dead loved ones and dresses them like servants
7-8	Natalia	Von Klaw	Collects fingernail clippings of monarchs and engraves herself on them
9-10	The Baroness Titania	of Scrodd	Defiles holy water for fun
11-12	Ludwig	Vollenveen	Compulsively paints pictures of women while they sleep
13-14	Dominique	Von Skorn	Serious mental problems – punches herself in the face under stress
15-16	Masha	The Grotesque	Addicted to white mushroom powder
17-18	Tamara	Gon Grolsch	Enjoys executions excessively
19-20	Octo	Ask	Has a peculiar fondness for injured women
21-22	Nadja	Korsk	Desires the throne at all costs
23-24	Clarissa	of Oog	Has no fingernails
25-26	Tyrnus	Von Vrogle	Compulsively shaves women bald
27-28	Gruntruck	of Vool	Once a spy for the Goblin City of Gaxen Kane
29-30	Yzonde	of Spyre	Fears to touch the ground
31-32	Kyle	Orzengork	Only finds joy in the sound of innocent women crying. Will go to extreme lengths to establish their innocence
33-34	Baron Vorgus	of Thrawl	Summons creatures from the lower planes for unsavory purposes
35-36	Cheswick	Bilious	Worships Groan, God of Despair
37-38	Lord Ascarious	Carn	Asexual
39-40	Jorgen	Orb	Despises the sound of the voices all around him, close to madness
41-42	Skorgen	Von Chasm	Only derives pleasure from others' fear
43-44	Vosulous	Eeben	Has a paralyzing fear of the Church of Vorn
45-46	Lady Frost	of Corg	Believes Vornheim to be a living entity hostile to her, but is afraid to leave
47-48	Enn Grath	of Orlac	Is possessed by the demon Belphegor
49-50	Sheera	of Zord	Bathes in the liquified bone of young maidens
51-52	Morgen	The Exquisite	Commits adulterous acts on a frozen lake as an offering to the moon goddess
53-54	Orrik	The Liar	Always tells the truth
55-56	Caustic	Von Bleak	Wants revenge on the Church of Vorn for unknown reasons
57-58	Cleopatra	of Thrasp	Addicted to hearing prophecies and predictions
59-60	Narska	of Asp	Wants to die but fears the underworld
61-62	Chrold	of Jordheim	Seeks to enslave the Wyvern of the Well
63-64	Hargen	the Cleaver	Fears to leave the city, for he is haunted by the squealing gnolls he has slain
65-66	Oskar	The Insidious	Is a permanently polymorphed goblin
67-68	Sasha	The Ogler	Is 8,000 years old, though she looks 14
69-70	Genevieve	of the Glove	Can speak, but hates her voice
71-72	Mazlowe	of Sklarr	Enslaved to a tentacled creature from the Isle of Oth hidden in his palatial home
73-74	Lilit	The Jewelled	Leads a secret second life as a dancing girl in the Eastern Quarter
75-76	Isabelle	DiArmond	Wants to kill her sister
77-78	Wolfgang	the Shrike	Surprisingly normal
79-80	Rotting Jane	of Greel	Has precognitive dreams
81-82	Unwerth	The Immense	Despises the sun
83-84	Grozgull	The Decapitator	Will only wear clothes of the recently deceased
85-86	Klaus	Griever	Compulsively steals small animals from the rest of the nobility and keeps them alive and hidden
87-88	Murgen	Von Vayle	Seeks the utter destruction of the city
89-90	Dusk	Von Hexen	Is a lich in desguise
91-92	Cordelia	Orq	Obsessed with aquiring the perfect shoes – will seek out the skin and bones of obscure creatures to aquire them
93-94	Lady Orchid	of Nexis	Believes that much of the nobility of Vornheim is in thrall to a creature from the lower depths
95-96	Ozgord	The Fearful	Is blackmailing several other NPCs for gold and favors
97-98	Osrick	of Raxxe	Keeps a small but powerful relic concealed inside his cane, but does not know how to activate it
99-00	Lord Rasping	of Hogg	Was in love with someone the PCs killed

Aristocrats

d%			
1-2	Controls spice trade from the East	Wears snow leopard fur and monocle	Married to...
3-4	Bribes maids for information on other Nobles	Black eyes, red robes	Sleeping with...
5-6	Breeds and trains the finest falcons on the continent	Short, bald, gruff, distracted	Father of...
7-8	Has finest art collection in Vornheim	Grinning, toothy, strangely attractive, alcoholic	Has rivalry with...
9-10	Collected powerful magical and occult items	Red-haired, scornful	A student of...
11-12	Expert in gems and jewels	One-eyed, wheeled around in a chair	Enamored of...
13-14	Owns majority of the best farmland on the continent	Intense, passionate, green-eyed	Worried about...
15-16	Breeds and trains the finest warhorses on the continent	Crude, jocular, skin missing near jaw	Works for...
17-18	Runs brothels all over the city	Rotund, elegant, sarcastic	Blackmails...
19-20	A recognized expert in the treatment of disturbed minds	Obsequious but piercingly intelligent	Suspects the truth about...
21-22	The cavalry of Vornheim is loyal to her above all others	Proud, pitiless, blue-eyed	Daughter of...
23-24	Owns the land beneath all the breweries on the continent	Mincing, meek, clever in business	Schemes with...
25-26	Expert in the intricacies of Vornheim law	Hairless, eager, awkward	Jealous of...
27-28	In charge of translations of foreign documents	Bow-legged, slow, talkative	Married to...
29-30	Child of the frost giant Queens of Nornrik	Limp, opulent, carried everywhere on a palanquin	Was once assaulted by...
31-32	Minister of Ratcatchers	Skulking, beady-eyed	Seeks aid from...
33-34	Level 15 wizard	Old, decrepit, almost immobile	Served by...
35-36	Minister of Imports and Licenses- oversees much of the administrative bureaucracy	Chubby, ruddy, bespectacled	Owes money to...
37-38	Commands a formidable army of animal breeders and mutators	Tedious, wheedling	Was gravely insulted by...
39-40	Court composer	Light, frivolous, ironic	Seeks the services of...
41-42	Royal exorcist	Dark-haired, wears baroque black armor	Exercises undue influence over...
43-44	Current regent of Vornheim	Wears bizarre ceremonial crown, weak voice, thin-fingered	Married to...
45-46	Wife of the regent, controls casual access to him	High-strung, middle-aged, pale	Enamored of...
47-48	Popular in society due to his elaborate and decadent masked balls	Gracious, intelligent, seemingly kind	Married to...
49-50	Important society tastemaker	Touchy, easily angered, fastidiously dressed	Is friends with but secretly schemes to destroy...
51-52	Charisma 18, enthralls nearly all who gaze upon her	Sentimental, fragile, dressed in silver & white silks	Married to...
53-54	Controls much of the trade in illicit substances in the city	Tells outrageous stories no-one believes	Trusts only...
55-56	Employs the finest chefs and cooks in Vornheim	Nervous, sweaty, sloppy	Married to...
57-58	"Queen of Riddles"- known for her mastery of obscure trivia	Open, honest, friendly	Friend of...
59-60	Is not native to Vornheim, travelled far and wide when she was younger and has stories of foreign lands	Brusque, intelligent, hunchbacked, aging	Lusts after...
61-62	Spymaster to the regent	Quiet, unassuming, tall	Has rivalry with...
63-64	Saved the city during the Battle of Ten Thousand Nights	Grim, warlike, unbending	Trusts only...
65-66	Skilled investigator, solved the murder of the last regent	Somber, patient, sympathetic	Annoys...
67-68	Charisma 18, Wisdom 18	Greedy, lusty, barbaric & blunt	Frequently employs...
69-70	Court portraitist	Always carries a glove, mute	Married to...
71-72	Physician to the regent	Protruding eyes, greenish veins, eerie	Lusts after...
73-74	Controls trade in cosmetics and important mining interests	Jewel-covered, vain	Sister of...
75-76	12th level cleric of White Web	Abrupt, impatient, wears long leather gloves	Seeks aid of...
77-78	Chief of the palace guard	Suspicious, excitable, hot-tempered	Married to...
79-80	Ambassador from Nornrik	Wary, detached, thin, aged and lame	Enjoys only...
81-82	Finest humorist in Vornheim- liked by nearly everyone. Collects jokes from around the world.	Fat, generous, bold, charismatic	Irritates...
83-84	Chief of the city's militia	Energetic, full of black humor	Friend of...
85-86	Chief adviser to the regent	Thin, wiry, creepy, long-nosed	Son of...
87-88	10th level witch	White-haired, talon-like hands, speaks in whispers	Is suspicious of...
89-90	A lovely child, beloved throughout Vornheim society	Radiant, buoyant, innocent, foolish	Adopted daughter of...
91-92	Major importer of silks and fabrics	Frivolous, forgetful, envious, insecure	Worries about...
93-94	Unimportant	Scarred, bitter, suspicious	Thinks no-one can help but...
95-96	All fear his power- his enemies are always exposed (or framed)	Greasy, fearless	Curious about...
97-98	Chief of cartography	Arrogant, devious, condescending	Trying to manipulate...
99-00	Renowned as an invincible duelist	Dark-eyed, clever, has three silver teeth	Works for... (01-02)

Books

Category	#	Topic
Books in foreign Languages (roll again to find topic, re-rolling results below 13)	1	Far East
	2	Goblin
	3	The 'Librarians' (Serpent people)
	4	Elf
	5	Nephilidian (or 'evil' species)
	6	White Elf (or other human noncommon)
	7	Gnoll
	8	Aquatic species
	9	Dwarf
	10	Halfling
	11	Dark Elf
	12	Mysterious
Biology, Zoology (may contain useful monster info)	13	General Biology
	14	Sea animals
	15	Reptiles
	16	Insects/arthropods
	17	Birds
	18	Mammals
	19	Unclassifiables/Unnatural Animals
Maps, Cartography (detailed works will be on any area GM has prepared)	20	City maps
	21	Local maps
	22	Maps of distant lands
	23	Ocean navigation charts
	24	Guides to cartography
	25	Travel guides/journals
Anatomy, Medicine	26	General Anatomy
	27	Diseases
	28	Durgery
	29	Medicinal herbs/potions
	30	Other treatments (applying leeches, moonbathing, etc.)
Magic (all texts useful for wizards might contain spells, texts useful to non-wizards will just help identify magical effects, curses, etc.)	31	Alchemy
	32	Summoning
	33	Enchantment
	34	Exorcism
	35	Necromancy
	36	Transmutation
	37	Illusion
	38	Divination
	39	Other or multiple disciplines
	40	Magical theory
	41	Demonology
Arts (d4: 1 – Theory, 2 – History, 3 – Technique, 4 – All Aspects) In large libraries roll d12 on this table to determine culture	42	Cosmetics
	43	Decorative arts
	44	Music
	45	Fiction
	46	Poetry
	47	Drama
	48	Architechure
	49	Painting
	50	Sculpture
	51	Puppetry
	52	Clothing

Category	#	Subject
Literature (roll d10 for quality, 10 is best) In large libraries roll d12 on this table to determine culture	53	Works of fiction
	54	Poetry
	55	Plays
	56	Literary nonfiction (essays, etc.)
	57	Jokes
Physical Sciences and Engineering	58	General physics
	59	Astronomy
	60	Chemistry
	61	Earth Sciences
	62	Meteorology
	63	Engineering manuals (general)
	64	Construction (buildings)
	65	Siege engines
	66	Armor and weapons
	67	Unusual and alchemical mechanisms
Botany	68	Flowers
	69	Trees
	70	Unusual, carnivorous and sentient species
	71	Herbs and other useful plants
Food and Drink	72	Cookbooks
	73	Wine
	74	Beer and Ales
	75	Other alcoholic beverages
	76	Food (general works)
	77	Agriculture
	78	Fishing
Mathematics	79	General works
	80	Algebra
	81	Geometry
	82	Extradimensional geometries
Religion (d4: 1-2 Commentaries 3-4 Sacred texts)	83	Titivilla (or god of healing)
	84	Gor (or god of law)
	85	Ch'od (or esoteric religion)
	86	Vorn (or other major religion)
	87	White Web (or evil cult)
	88	Other or nonhuman faith
Philosophy and Humanities (if 96 or 97, rolld12 on this table to determine language/culture)	89	General philosophical works
	90	Logic
	91	Ethics
	92	Law
	93	Political science
	94	Economics
	95	Linguistics
	96	Language manual
	97	Study of an alien culture
	98	Weapons and tactics
	99	Military history
	00	Military strategy

City NPCs

#	First	Last	Role	Description
1	Ott	Orben	Jester	Despises all life, is a secret sociopath, but drinks too much to get very far with it.
2	Jessika	Klove	One-legged...(roll again)	Helpful, frightened, likes fried food.
3	Rolf	Rechter	Travelling trader	Expert: local knowledge on some place the PCs haven't been yet but will probably get to before the end of the campaign. Suspicious but bribe-able.
4	Stielya	The Humble	Tavern keeper	Terrified of water. 4th level thief.
5	Werner	Brobe	King or lord in disguise	Wants to help the PCs because s/he's smitten with one of them. Possibly views other PCs as rivals.
6		Gruntruck	Grave digger	Desperately trying to sell some real estate- tavern, inn, weapons shop. Will accept ominously low price.
7	Chromula	Corgen	Child	Paranoid lycanthrophobe. Talks to on-one at night. Locks self up on full moons.
8	Albrecht	Gorbler	Grub-breeder	Amateur poet.
9	Blixa	Ringfinger	Suspicious, evasive weirdo	Alcholic idiot-savant thief.
10	Chastity	Glean	Pet groomer	Terrible prude. Will berate and shun anyone who appears to be having fun.
11	Madchen	The Mad	Thief	Fantastic barber. Doesn't know it.
12	Glister	Worg	Philosopher	Secret pervert. GM decides details.
13	Gor	Beak	Glassblower	From another plane.
14	Svetlana	Frozen	Long lost relative of PC	Scholar. Expert on first subject PCs happen to need information about while in his/her presence. Impatient and easily offended, however.
15	Valentina	Krone	Grain merchant	Always wants to help. Is kind of useless, though. Has an elaborately-carved sword (possibly magic).
16	Grendzel	Heuzengork	Dog-Catcher	2nd level fighter. Has terrible, communicable skin condition.
17	Ezerbet	The Harsh	Half-elven...(roll again)	Secretly a professional witchfinder. Probably somebody in the party qualified as a witch.
18	Orgun	Ash	Armorer	Radical democrat. Constantly trying to draw PCs into various regicidal schemes.
19		Horkenfreind	Jeweler	Reformed mad wizard (15th level). No longer casts spells. If the truth comes out and the PCs are very, very nice and reassuring, they may be able to persuade him/her to cast a spell, but each spell cast has a 10% chance of pushing him/her over the edge.
20	Valya	The Egregious	Singer	Is a random PC's mother in disguise.
21	Tatiana	Krawl	Pirate	Is secretly a creative genius on the level of William Shakespeare.
22	Nena	Eel	Nonhuman (GM chooses which)... (roll again)	3rd level fighter and hilarious! If PCs end up in a fight in which the NPC takes part (on either side), s/he will make quips. Roll Will save or under Wisdom to avoid laughing uncontrollably for d4 rounds.
23	Orchard	Underr	Architect	Inventor. Capable of coming up with mildly anachronistic tech. Sleeps too much.
24	Skrunweld		Half-Orc...(roll again)	Knows far more languages than anyone else. For reasons unknown.
25	Tasha	Vorvenveist	Knight	Is actually high-functioning neutral undead.
26	Tetra	Dreel	Drunk-almost unconscious- aristocrat	Gambler. A pretty good one actually. If the PCs can get on his/her good side they may catch some of the run-off from his/her post-winning spending sprees.
27	Vasken	Einen	Fetch-it girl/boy	Likes eating eggs. Has terrible asthma.
28	Illyana	Esk	Two goblins standing one on the other in human-shaped costume	Has constant, unaccountable, faux-European accent-drift. German one second, French the next, etc..
29	Klaw	Veert	Leatherworker	Wants to be a cleric very badly, isn't working out so well yet.
30	Unvelt	Umwelt	Executioner	Proud. Hungry for glory. Inept.
31	Porphyria	Zome	Hairdresser	Is nicknamed "The Hyena." The reason for this is, thus far, unclear...
32	Korgen	Kroner	Locksmith	Strength 18+. Has lice.
33	Zeera	Enzhyme	Confused foreigner	Inordinately fond of the halfing's pipeweed. Annoying. Wears sandals.
34		Geinheisenchast	Messenger	Ex-court jester. Not that funny. 1st level wizard.
35	Lolla	Mesmer	Carnival freak	Extremely insecure, addictive personality, whatever s/he's doing, s/he wishes s/he were doing soemthing else.
36	Ungrall	Unwern	Candlemaker	Has bizarre fungus colony growing in stomach. Knows it, and sings/recites poetry to it each night before going to bed. If slain, the colony will escape.
37	Throd	Throne	Builder	Was possessed once by a greater demon. Doesn't like talking about it. Blames self.
38	Hirgen	The Fondler	Fisherman	Extremely accommodating. Creepily accommodating. Will let the PCs stable their horses in his/her living room. Talks like Dracula. Totally harmless.
39	Ursula	Wiverne	Artist	Totally self-deluded, thinks s/he's very impressive and that the PCs are thoroughly impressed with him/her.
40		Hrundlefrust	Farmer	Forgetful. Narcoleptic. Handy.
41	Gundlee	Oaken	Brewer/Alewife	Local language isn't native language- always says "What is the word?...ahhhh..." Likes travelling.
42	Illona	Nadja	Alchemist	Has Machiavellian scheme of which every single thing that's occurred so far in the campaign is actually a part. Secret end of scheme is something unimaginably petty.
43	Ashen	Orngreen	Historian	Depressed, depressing, pessimistic, eerily lucky in all endeavors.
44	Olga	Krestle	Bowyer	Gourmet cook/chef/baker. Constantly trading or searching for exotic ingredients.
45	Rustveist		Militia Captain	Vomits often. No reason.
46	Myria	Zeelme	Engraver	Has an obscure cermonial obligation to do some strange but subtle ritual at dusk every day. May or may not actually prevent genuine dire mystical consequences.
47	Metta	The Inexhaustible	Tavern Wench	Carves chess peices when nervous. Isn't very good at chess. Plays for money, though.
48	Orv	Orm	Siamese twin (roll twice)	Extremely superstitious. Constantly seeking omens, signs, and luck charms. Some actually work
49	Hoarden	The Other Seer	Cleric	Amateur doctor. Takes scholarly interest in any disease.
50	Costly	Greasegraft	Doppleganger (roll again)	Can't read but likes to pretend s/he can.

#	Name	Epithet	Occupation	Description
51	Mestyvle	Myrn	Unemployed spouse	Never answers a question directly. If pressed, will cry.
52	Usher	Croon	Engineer	Unappreciated medieval art genius. Can do perspective and everything.
53	Misvet	Mourn	Even...(roll again)	Has an unusually well-maintained collection of dollhouses.
54	Fat Balto		Moneylender	Knows where to get the good lotus powder, has friends in all the guilds, all the local dancers owe him/her favors.
55	Fat Gorlo		Miner	Is disturbed by magic. Is trying to grow a beard. If s/he alreayd has one, is trying to decide whether to shave it.
56	Gasten	Skulk	Minstrel	Loves his/her job. Jolly and enthusiastic about it. May have Asperger's syndrome.
57	Mizten	Min Vale	Interpreter	Has fascinating theories about animal and monster behavior and something called "evolutionne threw natural selectionne."
58	Gristledown	Gorguts	Peddler	Fiercely devoted to random local deity. Was feircely devoted to rival local deity until fairly recently.
59	Sara	The Astonishing	Acrobat	Nervous. Knows secret weakness of important monster, but is probably too suspicious to tell anyone.
60	Wazi	Gruel	House painter	Angry amateur astrologer.
61	Greta	Gor Grothen	Dyer	Has a personal vendetta against most powerful NPC in campaign. Right-handed.
62	Velgo	The Pale	Navigator	Idealistically committed to racial harmony. Calls humans, elves, dwarves, etc. "demi-orcs." Has a wooden eye.
63	Grueling	Ungreen	Cartographer	Boring. Will talk until credibly threatened.
64	Griselda	Destruct	Playwright	Complains about minor physical ailments constantly. Ignores serious injuries or insults.
65	Raggi	The Inexplicable	Physician	Ferociously impatient. Interrupts everyone all the time.
66	Dinah	Grasp	Clothier	Swears constantly. Good at math.
67	Basil	The Slow	Soldier	Excellent hunter. Can find, kill, skin and gut a bear in seconds. Dislikes fighting otherwise.
68	Ovgrod	The Wretched	Baker	Has an entirely undeserved reputation as a lout in nearest city. Is actually quite charming.
69	Gretchen	Hargen	Cook	Charisma 18. Terribly charming. Enthusiastic for tales of adventure. Will trade information if the PCs tell him/her what they've been up to.
70	Oxnard	The Unctuous	Diplomat	Painfully stupid. Good-natured though. Always pretends like s/he knows what the PCs are talking about, but never does.
71	Rapunzel	Roth Resk	Juggler	Vegetarian. Fears the sight of blood. Has many foes.
72	Groast	Weever	Barrister	Is from a far more sophisticated culture far to the (east, south, whatever) and is sort of appalled and disgusted every time something medieval happens.
73	Vistula	Ohn	Servant	Inquisitive, intelligent, full of useful information.
74	Ferox	Grieve	Alchemist	Very sweet.
75	Arvik	Bleeve	Ratcatcher	Master spy. Has entirely opposite personality as s/he appears to have.
76	Greel	Gaster	Sailor	Eminently gullible and convincible- does what anyone tells him/her to do.
77	Ariska	The Crippled	Beggar	Locked in a Melvillean struggle with some monster/beast that haunts the city.
78	Anton	Fett	Scribe	Officious busybody. Secretly writes down information about everybody s/he's met.
79	Zsa Zsa	Van Vorn	Fishwife	Has obsessive compulsive disorder. Often feels uncontrollable urge to touch dangerous NPCs and monsters on the nose.
80	Constance	Voark	Apothecarist	Plays practical jokes. Lives with parents.
81	Suckling	Hoarder	Bookbinder	Has serious body-image problems. Keeps asking if s/he looks good in whatever s/he's wearing.
82	Deelia	The Whisperer	Gardener	Addicted to opium. Thinks PCs are a whole other group of PCs from a different campaign.
83	Esgreth	Orn	Carpenter	Claims to be son/daughter of a god— isn't.
84	Radinka	Weevil	Herbalist	Loves cat more than spouse.
85	Gustav	Groob	Furrier	Terrible with names. Makes up nicknames for everyone, forgets them, makes up new ones.
86	Chloris	Choke	Mercenary	Likes axes, mead, and fire.
87	Gorble	The Smiler	Astrology	Secretly carrying on a torrid love affair with another major NPC in the game.
88	Jasmine	Crumblecrust	Weaver	Has 25 children. Experiments with gunpowder.
89	Seskia	The Red	Storyteller	Knows the languages of animals. Not that they particularly like him/her.
90	Nordika	Vor Vorgen	Witch/Wizard	Secretly sells familiars on the black market.
91	Thyra	Valkyr	Hunter	Amateur psychiatrist- constantly trying to psychoanalyze the PCs whenever they meet. Fears pirates.
92	Eeben	Thrane	Innkeeper	Has a pet that isn't actually what s/he thinks it is.
93	Nyx	Blackbright	Fortune-Teller	Believes that crows despise him/her. Flees from them on sight. Ambidextrous.
94	Vermillion	Brasque	Lunatic	Never misses a chance to go to the theatre. Is often thrown out for brawling.
95	Borvalik	Wyrd	Shipwright	Has same tattoo as PC. If PCs are un-tattooed, has same father.
96	Izaster	Turnspine	Shoemaker	Is exactly like your favorite character from your favorite book only the opposite gender.
97	Brazz	The Rover	Dwarven...(roll again)	Has extensive war wounds. Hears things wrong a lot due to ear injury. Hilarity or disaster ensues.
98	Dita	The Clean	Spy	Feels no remorse. Has never seen the ocean.
99	Gorn	Whitewheel	Student	Will betray anyone who trusts him/her, then confess and beg for mercy. Enjoys beekeeping and horticulture.
00	Grosk	The Weeper	Stonecarver	Acts like a wise and omniscient mentor but is wrong all the time.

City Shopkeepers/Contacts

City Shopkeepers - Roll, pick, or just go in order as PCs meet merchants.

1. Fair prices, has a pet bird, will ask PCs if they ever had any pets.
2. Half blind, has a tough time valuing items, prices are fairly random, good selection though.
3. Greedy: buys low, sells high, is secret informant for police but sells info to anyone for right price.
4. Fat, funny, will talk your ear off, generous, likely to turn up dead in mysterious circumstances shortly after PCs interact with him/her.
5. Is surly, officious, religious, fair, gossipy, pumps all travelers for information about foreign lands and adventures, can be persuaded to buy drinks in exchange for stories or trade info for equally interesting info.
6. Old, wise, worldy, fond of women, good prices.
7. Organized, observant, possibly insane.
8. Keeps a monkey in his/her shop whom s/he despises, anyone kind to the monkey will be gouged, anyone cruel to the monkey will get great prices.
9. Wealthy, intelligent, bad prices, strange sense of humor, easily swayed by a pretty face.
10. Mute and illiterate, frequently comes into possession of unusual items and may offer them to the PCs though his descriptions and explanations (using an ad hoc sign language) are enigmatic.
11. Likes butterflies, collects butterflies, will trade goods for information in exchange for rare or exotic specimens, average prices.
12. Slow-moving, slow-thinking, dishonest, suspicious, expert at importing goods from remote or seemingly inaccessible areas.
13. Female dwarf, reserves a rare magic item and casks of fine honey mead for favored customers.
14. Troubled by strange dreams, accepts any interpretation no matter how bizarre, average prices.
15. One thousand pounds, rarely moves, former prostitute, terrible prices, good selection. Owns a vicious dog.
16. Fair prices, former assassin, rumored to posses a great deal of valuable information.
17. Is troubled by rats nibbling through his walls, is unaware that s/he is a wererat, not terribly bright, random prices.
18. Constantly distracted, always appears to be talking to unseen interlocutors, maybe just drunk all the time, fairly random prices.
19. Usually has the absolute best or worst prices in town, items are often stolen or faulty however s/he often has goods no one else does and is willing to buy things other merchants won't touch.
20. Exiled aristocrat from the West, usually begins with absurdly bad prices but can be haggled up or down fairly easily, vegetarian.

Contacts

1. Doesn't know.
2. Tells another interested party they were asking.
3. Gives wrong information accidentally.
4. "No but I can introduce you to someone who might..."
5. Says s/he doesn't know and seems afraid to say.
6. "No but you know who asked about that same thing..."
7. "Mmmmmmmayyybbbbeeee.... what's in it for me?"
8. "No but if you're interested in that, I have another proposition for you."
9. No but NPC has a vested interest in PCs finding the answer and will pay for it.
10. "Mmmm....maybe—let me see, can you come back tomorrow?" (When PCs come back, something has happened.)
11. Doesn't know but lets slip some piece of information that might be useful later on.
12. Knows!

Directions

CHA Check	Traditional Reaction Roll	Result
Succeed	8+	You get where you're going.
Fail by 1	7	You're lost, roll to see what neighborhood you end up in.
By 2	6	You're lost, roll to see what neighborhood you ended up in. Plus you're in a dark alley, there's a thief following you.
By 3	5	You're lost, roll to see what neighborhood you ended up in, plus roll a random encounter.
By 4	4	Refuses to give directions.
By 5	3	Refuses and is offended.
By 6 +	2	Person you're asking attacks you.

Connections Between NPCs

NPC 1 → NPC 2:
1. Married to...
2. Sleeping with...
3. Son/daughter of...
4. Hates...
5. Friends with...
6. In business with...

NPC 1 → NPC 3:
1. In criminal business with...
2. Friendly/ally of...
3. Created...
4. Once Saved...
5. Is Secretly...
6. Needs help from...

NPC 2 → NPC 3 (middle):
1. Once slept with...
2. Supplies...
3. Scares...
4. Has info about...
5. Is sweet on...
6. Respects...

NPC 4 → NPC 2:
1. Fate is entwined with...
2. Unwillingly shares power with,,,
3. Sleeping with...
4. Lusts after...
5. Suspicious of...
6. Secretly laughs at...

NPC 3 → NPC 4:
1. Once burned...
2. Owes money to...
3. Owes current circumstances to...
4. Cousin of...
5. Sleeping with...
6. Bribes...

Encounters

1-2	Troublesome drunk from a previous encounter (either in campaign or from PC's backstory).
3-4	Family member of recent victim of PC's recklessness/perfidity/righteous wrath (parents possibly of different races).
5-6	Damsel fleeing mutated thugs of wicked noble. Collapses at PC's feet.
7-8	Pickpocket attempting to steal important item from PC. If successful, thief runs to (Zoo of Ping Feng/Eshrigel's House/Library of Zorlac/Other Location), if not, clue to the theif's employer is on thief's body.
9-10	Winsome wench or dark-eyed youth. Encourages PC's to regale him/her with tales of adventure. Secretly feeds the details about PCs to accomplices—all thieves. They attack PCs one by one slowly after they scatter or sleep.
11-12	Scout for a decadent and fetishistic aristocrat charged with recruiting companions for his master precisely resembles PC's physical profile (athletic red-haird elf missing two teeth, etc.). Won't take no for an answer and has bodyguards.
13-14	Two well-dressed young men apparently helping a drunk friend home—in truth, he is dead. They ask the PCs to help them hide the body. They're working for (random noble) against (random noble) and demand total secrecy. Body was a courier delivering blackmail-worthy material to (second noble).
15-16	d10 escaped Face Rats— rats specially bred by envious courtiers to destroy the beautiful. They will attack eyes, noses, ears, etc. Alchemical element in their saliva prevents facial wounds from fully healing. The hp damage can be healed but the disfiguring effects can only be cured by Remove Curse or similar magic.
17-18	Husky, green-eyed dog begins following party member.
19-20	*PCs stumble into the middle of a street fight or tavern brawl between (d8) 1—Young lords of a noble house 2— Criminal gang 3— Berserkers 4— Church faction 5— Cult 6— Party of adventurers 7—Strange beast 8— Seemingly harmless group (old women, cripples, etc.) who fight with unexpected ferocity and...(roll d8 again).
21-22	*Common pickpocket.
23-24	Pregnant woman missing tooth starts argument, accuses party member of mistreating her. Local militia responds.
25-26	Street/floor collapses, d6 PCs tumble 50 feet into black water and stone tunnels. Strange toads (or albino crocodiles encrusted with jewels) stir in the murk.
27-28	Group of thieves strike in well-coordinated ambush, using decoys, crossbows, backstabs, etc.. Saves or checks should be allowed to possibly see it coming.
29-30	d8 tentacles erupt from corpse or carcass in street and strike. Footman in livery lurks nearby during the encounter, pays everyone involved 50 gp to remain silent about the incident then makes his way back to his employer's home.
31-32	*Unusually fierce wind and snow. Outside vision is obscured, movement's halved, and missile attacks are at -5 for the next 12 hours. Commerical establishments have 3 times the usual number of customers (weather refugees) and these are of a wider swath of social classes than usual.
33-34	Merchant recognizes martial and battle-scarred bearing of PCs and quietly offers them battered but functional siege tower in working condition concealed in warehouse a few blocks away for only 300 gp.
35-36	*District's citizens are in midst of lottery festival. Will not allow PCs through unless they participate. Each participant is randomly assigned a fate for one month: example—s/he is considered a slave of another charater, s/he is treated as if s/he were a different person for a month, s/he must steal a white mask from a tall tower, s/he is considered ritually invisible and must be ignored, etc.
37-36	City enters Enigmatic Phase due to rare atrological conditions. Distances distort, effects precede causes, strange alleys and streets leading to hitherto unknown parts of city appear. All things subtly dreamlike for two hours. Longtime residents have been through this before.
39-40	Mercenaries returning after campaign in the East. One spoil is long lost friend of PC's who quietly beseeches him/her for aid as s/he is paraded past in 4 foot cage and taken to a prison, knight's home, or marketplace.
41-42	Thieves employing minor magics. Each PCs must save vs spell or be lost and seperated from the group. d6+2 3rd level thieves then attack—trying for at least one theif per PC.
43-44	Lunar eclipse. Citizens become nervous, superstitious, and paranoid until next morning.
45-46	PC is accused of violating a local sumptuary law because of some item of clothing s/he is wearing. Militia attempts to arrest PC.
47	Drunk fortune teller pronounces three fates, unasked (see Fortunes, page 56.)
48-49	*Driving rain. Everyone is at -2 to anything involving balance or visibility for the rest of the day.
50	Criminals sabotage wall of ropeworks as distraction while attacking nearby target. All passing must save or take damage from boiling hogfat.
51-52	Gang of drunken berserkers accosts PCs looking for an excuse to fight.
53	Powerful noble of opposite sex aggressively purues PC (probably one w/highest Charisma), will be offended if refused.
54	Due to long-ago alchemical experiment, area PCs pass through is infused with chaotic magical forces during certain phases of the moon. Attempts to use magic in area will go haywire in an interesting way. Wizards may be allowed roll to sense this.
55	Troupe of viciously persistent street clowns demand some form of social justice. Exhort PCs to join their cause— they will follow the PCs, juggling and performing small magic tricks until driven away by force.
56-57	*Ice. All are at -4 to anything involving balance for the rest of the day.
58	Desperate relative demands aid in escaping local gang s/he's offended/crossed/cheated.
59-60	Trained monkey pickpocket. Possibly disguised as entertainer.

#	Encounter
61	Shrieking fungus spores have escaped wild garden or alchemist's lab and float through air. PC save vs poison or shriek wildly for 3 rounds whenever touched for next 2 days.
62	Disguised goblin kidnappers. Will attempt to capture PCs, drag them to hidden lair in city and interrogate PCs about the city's defenses and random mundane details of human life. Their leader has a pet crocodile.
63	Party passes members of Princeling Gang buying white moth opium off gang of smugglers. Both sides are inclined to kill PCs to avoid being exposed.
64	Party passes noblewoman being assaulted by cutthroats— they attack the party to avoid being identified.
65-66	*Night market or festival. Roll d4 as the PCs wade through: 1—pickpocket 2—trained monkey pickpocket 3—gang of toughs looking for fight 4—Attractive NPC asks PC to win toy for him/her
67	*Gang of theives armed with green mold powder bomb. Bomb is thrown first— save vs. poison or be confused for 2 rounds. d4+2 thieves then attack.
68-69	Desolate street d10 wolves gnaw on something in doorway
70-71	*Thieves attack from above. One swings down on a line, stabs party member, and is hauled up quickly through window on other side of street by comrades. d6 others come in from surrounding alleys.
72-73	Desolate street. Victim of recent assault lies bleeding in street (roll random City NPC page 50). Will be grateful for aid.
74	Desolate street. Apparent victim of recent assault lies bleeding in the street. Is actually armed robber and will strike when turned over— as will d6 fellow thieves.
75-76	Travelling thieves disguised as street performers. They have attracted enough of crowd to block street and d4 sneak through crowd pickpocketing while others perform.
77-78	Doivel and Spoyt, powerful and notorious pair of overweight brothers obscurely connected with theatre industry wallow in gutter, wearing opera clothes and smiling. Wave pleasantly and tipsily to party. Will reappear at margin of PC's lives— for good-or-ill -- from now on, depending on how they are treated at this moment.
79	Expensively-dressed middle-aged couple having shrieking argument in street. Man: "You are naught but a STRUMPET! Wayward and deceitful!" Woman: "A strumpet? (turns to party) Do I look like a strumpet to you?" (She will demand an answer.) Either will be a steadfast friend if party takes their side and a constant foe if opposed. Both are (secretly) 4th-level wizards
80	Quiet street. Party notices beggar stuffing entire granary cat into his mouth alive. Every subsequent time party passes this way they will notice beggar growing fatter and fatter. He faintly radiates magic. Demon of the 4th type is attempting to prepare beggar's body so it can manifest itself through him. If left unmolested for 2 months, now-enormous beggar will have abilities and disposition of the demon
81	PCs and passing nun arrive just in time to see victim being decapitated by a lone theif. Nun warns that if PCs don't help catch the thief, victim will return as a Headless (some kind of undead—GM decides) and hunt them all down one by one, starting with the thief. She's right.
82	A messenger in livery staggers out of an alley bleeding and drops dead at the PC's feet holding up message for powerful alewife Dolphia Sternborg concerning a caravan containing a massive shipment of hops (held up during a detour through the Spine mountains). If the PCs do nothing, the price of beer and ale quickly spikes to 50 gp and panic spreads.
83	Peasant revolt or mass religious lunacy— torches wave, effigies burn. This part of the city will be crowded and distracted for the rest of the night.
84	Someone sneezes on a PC and apologizes. The virus thus communicated is semisentient. It wants the PC to: A) be around other people, B) be ill but not dead, and C) pass on its own genetic material. It will therefore periodically encourage the PC to engage in behaviors which advance these goals. PC must save to avoid agreeing with the voice inside his/her head's suggestions. Once per day until a save is failed, then once per hour, then once every five minutes, then once a round.
85	PC notices one of the group of older, distinguished-looking gentlemen wearing or holding something recently stolen from a PC or something s/he recognizes as belonging to a prominent harmless NPC.
86	PCs notice a frightened and wild-eyed girl run past, one arm dyed blue— marking her as an inmate at a lunatic asylum. A block or two later they'll notice another dyed fugitive, and then another. A powerful inmate has engineered a mass escape.
87	A juggler (Charisma 18) asks the crowd to throw him something--anything— and he'll juggle it, along with 6 flaming torches. Someone grabs something off the slowest PC and tosses it to him. The juggler's actually a pretty nice guy.
88	Desperate-looking messenger presses 1' x 1' box into a PCs hand and begs him/her to hide it and s/he'll get it later, then runs off. It contains a glass aquarium with a removable top. It's full of water, and swimming inside are tadpole-sized sperm (many colors). They are from a random selection of species. Any egg of any kind placed in the tank will be fertilized by one of them and produce a bizarre hybrid that will grow to maturity in 3 days.
89	Handful of people abusing a goblin or other obvious non-local. S/he is actually a desperate envoy from a peace-loving faction attempting to notify Vornheim of a coming invasion from his/her citystate.
90-91	A nightingale is perched on a corpse. It is the nightingale from the Immortal Zoo (pg 20). It is hunting for a mate. something shiny a PC is carrying has caught its eye. It will attempt to steal it and bring it back to the Zoo. If the nightingale from the Zoo is dead, it is the nightingale's mate, observing the PCs and plotting revenge.
92	A PC begins to hear whispers whenever s/he is outside. These whispers are from one of the 10,000 wind gods. He is trapped in the Library, Zo, Eshrigel's House, or somewhere else in the city by a powerful NPC. The god wants to be freed and, to this end, will give the PC advice or directions necessary to free him. He may only whisper one word every 10 minutes though.
93	Most attractive and desirable NPC a PC has ever seen. Random occupation, random personality, currently embroiled in a random legal situation.
94	3rd leve Cleric kneeling and howling "Why? Why has thou forsaken me?????" into the wind. S/he will become a formidable and horrifying evil cleric if nobody convinces him/her of the truth and righeousness of Vorn's judgement sometime in the next day.
95-96	Neighborhood celebrating the Festival of Effigies. People replace themselves with scarecrow-like life-sized dolls made of fabric and children wack them with sticks for the candy and goat cheeses inside.
97	8 freshly-baked custards spill out of the back of a pompous and imposing carriage bound for the palace and are miraculously unharmed. The custards are worth 500 gp each but only if sold fresh (in the next few hours) and to the right buyers. Few buyers would buy more than one.
98-99	A tarot card reading finds a passing PC alluring and offers to tell all the PCs fortunes for free. Roll fortunes as usual, except a roll of 50 means the Devil has been pulled, and the PC will soon face a demon, 00 will indicate the 4 of cups has been pulled and the PC will soon face a vampire, two PCs getting the same results indicates The Moon has been chosen and a werewolf is coming, and 23 will indicated Death and the PCs will soon face a litch. The cartomancer is smitten and will follow the PC around if encouraged even slightly.
00	Devoted servant mistakes PC for his long-absent master. Is overjoyed to see PC/. Will bring him/her to a massive, lavish towertop residence and give him/her the key. (This does not count as treasure for the purpose of XP, though any subsequent money made by peruptuating this ruse does).

Fortunes

1	You will narrowly escape death by water.
2	The one you fear will wear a disguise.
3	A joke will cost you a treasured possession.
4	Something blue will hurt you at dusk.
5	You will deceive someone in the marketplace using a ferret.
6	Follow the crow to find the way.
7	You will see a bridge collapse, but not completely.
8	A tear will be shed for you in an unexpected quarter.
9	A reptile will bring you three objects.
10	A fierce rain will interrupt a search for a gleaming object.
11	A wooden wheel will turn out to be made of stone.
12	A stray quail will bring hungry dogs.
13	You will spend two days in darkness, meeting no-one.
14	A feast will be prepared, but not eaten.
15	You will be ignored for 3 minutes by someone wearing a hat.
16	A child will deliver a message for you.
17	You will light a torch and then hear a terrible howling.
18	An axe will land in the throat next to yours.
19	A dark passageway will turn out to be a figment of your imagination.
20	Cold claws will seize you, and you will weep.
21	You will fall through ice, and into a wall.
22	You will be mistaken for a biscuit.
23	A calculation made in secret will be unreliable.
24	Three blades will meet in mid-air.
25	A boulder will tumble sidelong into a thief before your eyes.
26	One who is ill will be ill twice more.
27	A rope will snap as music plays.
28	An early breakfast will be interrupted by lava.
29	A horse and a fat man will appear simultaneously.
30	A crown will roll across a stone floor.
31	The weather will change your life, twice.
32	A red eye will go blind.
33	Careless treatment of livestock will lead to a quick death.
34	You will see a blind goat and a singing star.
35	A game of cards will lead to an erotic encounter.
36	A lock will prove unreliable.
37	A spherical object will make you laugh.
38	A fish will swim in a pearl-colored pool.
39	A night will take three days to pass.
40	An item of clothing will be revealed to be full of weevils.
41	A spider will speak to you after tasting marmalade.
42	You will be impaled on a summer evening.
43	A gold ring will roll between a pair of floorboards.
44	You will witness a murder in a quiet garden.
45	You will win a race by losing a meal.
46	You will find shelter in a carcass.
47	You will see a broken clock in a lonely tower.
48	A foreigner will trust you immediately.
49	You will be set on fire.
50	Drowning elves will beg you for mercy.

51	An ogre will mock your request.
52	You will touch a wild boar twice.
53	A plague will slay 10,000 bards and none will weep.
54	A prayer will be answered by the wrong god.
55	You will seize power through flattery, and lose it through gluttony.
56	You will gain a friend by performing a coin trick.
57	Your death will free seven prisoners.
58	You will see a statue crumble, and none will reassemble it.
59	An unshaven hermit will die to defend you.
60	A woman will be cruel to you three times, and kind once.
61	You will see a criminal die with fruit in his mouth.
62	Fog will obscure passage through a ruined port.
63	You will win the favor of a barbaric woman.
64	You will be given a message by a strange man carrying a spoon.
65	You will be given a spoon by a strange man carrying a message.
66	You will be given a slow and searching look, and then be thrust through a door.
67	You will win a contest that you thought you'd lost.
68	You will be obeyed by one who mocks you.
69	The size of your nose will be discussed.
70	A window will shatter silently.
71	A stag will leave a trail of blood but none will notice it.
72	A poor man will be mistaken for a rich one, and a rich one will be mistaken for a woman.
73	A crude drawing will disturb you.
74	You will be separated from a companion, and be reunited by a malfunctioning device.
75	What remains of your family will be slain while you deliver a message.
76	An arrow will pierce your thigh and land in a useful place.
77	A child's toy will turn out to have a sinister purpose.
78	You will enter a fortress hidden in a carpet.
79	You will successfully blackmail a man eating pheasant.
80	You will decapitate the wrong wizard.
81	You will be swallowed while you sleep.
82	You will be impersonated by a bald man.
83	A tower will crumble after you eat four meals inside.
84	One you hoped to surprise will be expecting you, and one you love will be on fire.
85	A key will be discovered in an enemy's sock.
86	A tired man will offer to take you to the theatre.
87	You will have a terrible headache after shedding orcish blood.
88	You will learn a delicious recipe from a beared woman.
89	You will forget to check the ceiling.
90	One you seek will be found in a closet.
91	You will receive credit for something you did by accident.
92	You will meet a beggar who resembles you in every way.
93	You will inspire fear in a man with one eye.
94	You will remember something important while drunk.
95	A gnome will offer to buy you shoes.
96	A jealous lover will give you a magnet.
97	A hideous creature will stumble on a bucket.
98	A tedious pedant will act as your translator.
99	An avalanche will ruin your evening.
00	You will find a clue in an earring just after losing a toe.

"I Search the Body"

1-3	*Flask.
4-5	*Random book.
6-7	*Hastily-drawn map leading from one place in the city to another.
8-57	*Number of gp equal to d100 roll just thrown.
58	Engagement ring and semi-literate drafts of marriage-proposal speech with name of potential fiancé written in margins.
59	Recipe for scones.
60	Elephant's tusk knife.
61	Draft of new law forbidding beer, dancing, and/or public-speaking among the lower classes throughout Vornheim, not yet signed.
62	Deed of sale for a plot of land, signed, revealing that a very large or important part of the city is now in the hands of an NPC known to be shady.
63	Deed of sale for an artwork (signed), suggesting the artwork's value to the new owner is vastly out of proportion to its size and quality.
64	Sketches, clearly from life and by a talented hand, depicting daughter of a noble house in compromising positions.
65	An unusual fish with a single green eye, carefully wrapped, as if for delivery.
66	Device the size of a pocket watch containing inlaid images of clouds, suns, etc. capable of predicting the weather one day ahead of time.
67	Journal, seemingly written in a calligraphic style characteristic of the scriptoria of the Eminent Cathedral, seething with heretical ideas.
68	Exotic blue egg, carefully wrapped in a map leading to an icy cliff miles from the city.
69	Crushed fairy/brownie/pixie/leprechaun.
70	Ivory belt buckle shaped like a horse.
71	¼ of a candle-eel. (see Buildings on the Inside Back Cover)
72	Stale piece of bread.
73	*Pair of dice.
74	Loaded pair of dice.
75	Small mirror.
76	Satirical deck of cards depicting political figures of 10 years ago.
77	Locket containing a small engraving of a seemingly-unrelated NPC of a completely different social class.
78	Gold statuette of a two-headed piglet. Is actually a real bicephalic piglet encased in gold stolen from Zoo of Ping Feng and will remain immortal so long as it is encased.
79	Beautiful continental map from 900 years ago. Contains locations of long-forgotten empires, including ones once located where the PCs are.
80	Looks similar to healing potions but it's actually a love potion. Drink it and fall in love with whoever last wounded you.
81	Ceremonial silver knife with a Bishop of Vorn carved into the pierced blade. Specifically consecrated for an assassination attempt on the bishop by a mysterious cult.
82	Small carved figurine or chess piece of one of the PCs, precise in every detail, 25-28mm tall. Purpose unknown.
83	d10 x 100 living snails with specially-made shells cast from pure silver worth 1 sp. Snails are sentient, communicate telepathically, and will beg PCs not to trade them away.
84	Assortment of 10 gems apparently worth d4 x 10 gp total, 5 are cursed (each in a different way), 5 bless the owner with magical properties (each in a different way). The 5 curses are precisely the opposite of the 5 bonuses and they cancel each other out. Getting rid of any one of the gems will cause its opposite to take effect on the owner.
85	Parts of a small copper golem, about 2 feet tall when assembled. If both blood and tears touch it, golem will attack the one whose blood is spilled on it with the abilities of the one whose tears were spilled on it.
86	Small, elaborately carved stone sphere (or wheel) the size of a baseball. If any being larger than a cat is shrunk by magical means and placed inside the ball or wheel and begins to move, the creature becomes unstoppable— able to roll through walls and obstacles as if they were cobwebs.
87	A small vial of blue dust, breathing it causes victim to forget the last hour.
88	Tiny scale model of an ordinary tower in Vornheim. Opening or closing the model's doors and windows causes the corresponding part of the real building to open or close.
89	Vial containing the digestive juices of the dreaded rust beast.
90	Seed of a species of sentient, mobile tree.
91	Skull of gnoll in silver and ebony— actually a reliquary designed to mount and display the tooth of a gnollish saint.
92	Coins that eat other coins in the dark. This causes the coin to grow, but not large enough to compensate for the value of the lost coins.
93	Like a jeweled comb but has three 6-inch tines set into a triangular base, used for arranging a mesdusa's "hair".
94	Set of 12 small translucent, colored cubes that, when dropped in a body of water, produce a variety of different effects— bubbles, color change, soothing steam, pleasant hallucinations, etc.
95	Vial of "Mirror Water". When spilled, the puddle is a portal to a 'looking glass' dimension. If anyone attempts to walk across the puddle, an exact duplicate of themselves (same abilities, equipment, etc.) will crawl out and attempt to kill them.
96	Change of socks.
97	*Piece of cheese.
98	Toy horse with wheels.
99	Letter of introduction to a major local cleric extolling NPC's virtue and honesty.
00	Glass-cutting tool.

Legal Situations

1	Trial by combat d4: (1-2 Tittivillan law: unarmored duel with severed goat horns) (3-4 Vorn's law: combatants up to their waists in rusty water.)
2	Trial by jury of people who know the defendant well. Local militia assigned to bring in individuals who have known the defendant for years and will travel great distances if necessary to find them. The number of juror should equal (however many members of the PC party would count as jurors) +5 more. Trial does not start until jurors can be found.
3	Defendant is thrown of a cliff into an icy fjord. If s/he survives, s/he's innocent.
4	Ordinary trial but judge is half-deaf and farcically drunk. May make snap rulings based on half-understood arguments.
5	Ordinary trial but one witness is actually dozens of organisms, nested one inside the next like a Russian doll. If anyone can discover this and the magical means of "opening" the witness, all the "nested" witnesses will testify to the same facts.
6	Defendant is set loose and allowed to run for an hour. A 'sanctuary stone' is hidden somewhere in the district. If the defendant can reach it before the milita can reach him/her, s/he is declared innocent.
7	Trial by drama: all involved must play themselves in a pair of improvised dramas re-enacting the events of the day/night in question in one of Vornheim's great theaters before a jury/audience of thousands. Each depicts one side's version of events. Most convincing play wins, audience decides by applause.
8	Defendant faces those who arrested him/her in fair combat. However, the secret goal is to prove that the defendant was brought in by divine providence rather than by superior force-- therefore if the defendant defeats hi/her captor-- thus proving s/he is a superior fighter-- it proves s/he was meant to be captured. The only way to be set free is to lose the combat, thus proving the defendant was only caught because of the skill of the pursuer.
9	Trial by jest: Defendant and accuser mock one another's positions before a wizened jury of seemingly humorless elders. Funnier one wins.
10	Trial by demon: The rarest system and considered the fairest— occasionally clerics will capture and imprison a minor demon believed to be responsible for some class of crime (burglary, extortion, etc.). The demon is asked if the defendant committed the crime and ritually compelled to tell the truth. Whether the clerics in question have any idea what they're doing is the GM's choice.
11	Trial by swine: The people of Vornheim believe pigs to be the only honest animals. 7 pigs are tied to the defendant by 10' ropes and the defendant must go about his or her business in this way for 12 days. If the defendant cuts the ropes, leaves the city, or goes mad s/he is guilty.
12	Biographical trial: PC must recite his or her life story to the jury. If they judge him/her to be a good and useful person, s/he goes free. They may ask questions.
13	Trial by pie: The defendant and prosecutor have 24 hours to prepare as many pies (1 foot diameter) as possible. The accuser then consumes any of his/her pies as quickly as possible. The defendant must then consume any one of his/her own pies as fast or faster. The accuse then must eat any one of the defendant's pies as fast as that or faster, and then vice versa and then the sequence starts over until one party or the other is unable to finish a pie in time (and therefore loses) or runs out of pies (and therefore loses). The winner is entitled to any and all remaining pies.
14	Defendant is presumed guilty and must "prove the demon of the crime has passed to another host" by catching someone else committing the same kind of crime within 3 days. S/he is assigned a pair of militiamen both to insure s/he does not flee and to aid in the pursuit.
15	Fifty randomly chosen citizens are brought to the courthouse along with as many friends of the accuser and defendant as they can muster. The defendant and accuser then duel to the death, held aloft by the crowd. If either touches the ground before the other is dead, s/he loses.
16	Trial by seduction. Citizens unknown to the defendant are invited to a brief hearing wherein both sides make arguments. Each citizen secretly notifies the court of their personal verdict and then, if they are strongly moved one way or the other, attempts to seduce the defendant (who is set free but kept under observation) over the course of the following weeks. If the defendant's favors are first won by one who thinks him/her innocent, s/he is set free, if by one who thinks him/her guilty, s/he is convicted. If both simultaneously, s/he is innocent. If s/he remains celibate for one month, a new form of the trial is selected.
17	Trial by assassin. 20 citizens unknown to the defendant are invited to a brief hearing wherein both sides make arguments. The defendant is freed, but kept under observation. Each citizen secretly notifies the courst of their personal verdict and, if they believe the defendant guilty, may attempt to kill the defendant over the course of the next 2 months. If the defendant survives (slaying the assassins is permitted, but only if they thought the defendant guilty), s/he is considered innocent.
18	Trial by proxy combat. 3-6 friends of the defendant and an equal number of official judicial assassins attempt to kill each other. First side to kill every member of the opposition wins. If anyone on either side leaves the city, that side loses. The defendant can't fight but can give advice.
19	Anti-trial: Some friend of the defendant is legally bound to masquerade as his lawyer and attempt to persuade an unknowing jury that the defendant is guilty while the accuser must attempt to prove the defendant innocent. If the verdict is guilty, the defendant is considered innocent and vice versa. This practice is believed to increase sympathy for those with opposing points of view.
20	Two animals of different kinds in the district (often a toad and a weasel) are selected. The defendant must convince the jury that the first animal committed the crime of which s/he has been accused and the accuser must convince the jury that the second animal did. If the defendant is found to be more convincing, s/h is innocent, otherwise, s/h is convicted.

Magic Effect

1-2	Two targets melded together like conjoined twins.
3-4	Reverse crowd's value system—deosn't compel action but may allow casters to steal publicly, etc.
5-6	Coincidence curse, victim keeps randomly meeting people s/he has offended.
7-8	Hole appears in floor leading to next level down or subterranean tunnel. Hole persists for length of spell.
9-10	Target smells and tastes good— attracts carnivorous species.
11-12	Zero gravity.
13-14	Small wolf's head appears on object or on caster's hand, capable of vicious bite (as wolf).
15-16	All animals, including pets or animal companions, hate targets.
17-18	Target cursed— will spoil all food and drink within 10' radius.
19-20	Target shrieks uncontrollably when touched for 10 minutes.
21-22	Next time target touches a wall, s/he is held fast by an unseverable bond.
23-24	Random target limb auto-amputates, however, at the end of the spell's duration limb will attempt to seek out its owner and, if successful, will reattach itself. Condition is contagious for length of spell.
25-26	Target's voice becomes unimaginably shrill and irritating.
27-28	Target sees ghosts of all who died in this spot. Failed save will cause fear but a successful one may allow target to acquire useful information about the past.
29-30	Target cannot stand the taste of food— an effort of will (saving throw) must be made during every meal in order to eat.
31-32	Target becomes preternaturally gluttonous--an effort of will (savings throw) must be made to avoid eating any item s/he can see or smell.
33-34	Children despise target.
35-36	Terrible weather follows target.
37-38	One of caster's eyes emerges from his/her eye socket on spider-like legs as the caster flees. Eyespider has 1 HD but can cast spells as if it were the wizard. (If effect is not from a caster, a 1 HD spellcasting eye simply emerges).
39-40	Target's toes auto-amputate and become maggots, biting the target, balance becomes difficult (saving throw or Dexterity check). Toes reattach and become normal when spell ends.
41-42	Victim's mouth begins to migrate across and around his/her body. At 10th level the mouth does not return to its proper location when the spell ends.
43-44	Caster's body splits in half, each able to function normally and possessing half the original number of hit points. By touching a target while in this state, a half-caster may similarly split a foe. A successful grapple allows a half-caster to meld his/her body with the target's and use all of their abilities.
45-46	Curse: everything target touches turns to glass for length of spell.
47-48	Target's tongue becomes a viper's head. Automatically bitten for d4 + poison on inside of mouth each round. May attempt to bit it off but this is dangerous.
49-50	Spellcasting target discharges one of his/her spells in manner of the caster/GM's choosing.

51-52	All intelligent creatures find target ridiculous/laughable
53-54	All intelligent creatures find target pathetic
55-56	Small dog appears inside target's body. d12 damage per round until it is removed.
57-58	Curse: All liquids make target drunk.
59-60	Target's body inflates to 6' in diameter, target can move at 1/3rd speed and is at -4 to attack. Takes 1hp damage per point of armor.
61-62	Caster spits a small black toad into the air, which lands on a target within 15'. Toad attacks (in the same round) as a 5 HD monster, if successful, the toad bites the target for d8hp and target will vomit up another toad (still in the same round) which will leap at the next available target (within 15') and attack in the same way and with the same consequences. The process continues until one of the toad's attacks is unsuccessful. Toads dissolve into an inky black goo at the end of the round.
63-64	Curse: Target rusts all objects within 3' for the duration of the spell (at least an hour).
65-66	Target performs exact opposite of desired action on a d6 roll of 5 or 6 (roll each round).
67-68	Target powerfully magnetized, all unsecured metal objects within 20' fly toward target.
69-70	Target blinds anyone who hears his/her voice for 10 minutes. Caster excepted.
71-72	Target fears all spherical objects or creatures.
73-74	Target moves through normal air as if through water. Target is affected as if slow but the victim may "swim" up or down.
75-76	Target can't see wolves (or goblins, or other common dangerous species in campaign).
77-78	Target switches positions with caster (or object).
79-80	Caster's body turns to living tar-like substance— cutting, thrusting and piercing weapons lodge harmlessly in it. Objects must be removed before effect ends or caster dies.
81-82	Geometry becomes non-Euclidean in 40' radius— everyone is at -d6 to hit, anything moving appears in random location within the affected area.
83-84	Part of target's mind possessed by minor demon-- discussion of a certain subject causes demon to take control for d4 rounds — roll on random book chart (pg 48) to determine subject.
85-86	Curse: Target must eat his/her weight in gold each day in order to survive.
87-88	Target takes damage whenever caster/object does.
89-90	Alternating spellplague: target affected by *Irresistible Dance* spell, closest intelligent lifeform within 10 feet of dancer is affected by *Uncontrollable Laughter* spell, next closest intelligent lifeform within 10' of laughter affected by Irresistible Dance spell, etc.
91-92	Common word cursed ("I", "is", etc.). Every time target hears that word s/he is afflicted by *Uncontrollable Laughter* spell.
93-94	Target's facial features change— species and sex are unchanged but everything else is different-- and continue to change every minute thereafter.
95-96	Target's head turns 180° around, facing backwards.
97-98	Target's abilities are reversed— his/her chances of doing everything are opposite. Must roll the opposite of what s/he must normally roll to succeed.
99-00	Target won't stop talking about the moon.

Taverns and Games

d20	Name	Name	Games	Other Notes
1	Howling	Wench	Grubfights	The boar's head hanging over the bar secretly knows the common tongue.
2	Shrieking	Hog	Darts	A storyteller often visits, singing songs of local rogues, spreading news of their deeds.
3	Tainted	Cudgel	Billiards	A key to the library of Zorlac (or other improbable place) is hidden in the 9-ball.
4	Grotesque	Troglodyte	Sting	Frequented exclusively by bored and arrogant nobles in preposterous costume.
5	Broken	Beetle	Drinking Contests	One of the serving girls is a 3rd level theif. One table was once a sentient tree.
6	Frigid	Moon	Arm Wrestling	A daughter of a vicious noble is hiding from her parents, working as a serving girl.
7	Icy	Beaver	Boxing	Kidnapper/recruiters working for gladiatorial promoters occasionally skulk about.
8	Fizzing	Stone	Toss	The bartender's pet ferret is a polymorphed wizard. He doesn't know.
9	Bleak	Queen	Large Chess	Expensive. The cruelest barons of Vornheim come here to hatch their schemes.
10	Harmless	Crow	Pin the Serpent	Far out on the arm of a half-crumbled bridge 150' above a quiet square.
11	Busy	Wife	Eye Spitting	Organized vertically around a spiral staircase. Rare snails crawl the walls.
12	Bell &	Bone	Darts, Grubfights	Eshrigel the medusa's daughter is often found here, drinking whiskey.
13	White	Adder	Basilisk Fights	Extremely exclusive. Drunk wizards are occasionally found mumbling in the corners.
14	Knife &	Needle	Truth or Challenge	Countertops of copper and zinc. Frequented by poets and anarchists.
15	Fond	Cousin	Trivia	Owner runs a smuggling ring. Light crossbows and shortswords behind the bar.
16	Huge	Elephant	Flaming Chess	Cheap. The best food in Vornheim. Owner has three trained wolves.
17	Scorned	Weasel	Devilswheel	Frequented by thieves. Cheapest fare in Vornheim. Secret door to tunnel to cathedral in basement.
18	Cup &	Claw	Joke Contest	Serves candies with oracular messages inside. Criminals occasionally communicate via these candies.
19	Ghastly	Orb	Floating Sting	Flooded shoulder-deep. Scantily-clad serving wenches walk through the water, holding trays above the surface. Tables and chairs are set into cylindrical wells to keep the patrons dry. Exclusive and expensive.
20	Hunting	Hare	Eating Contests	A rival gang to the Fond Cousin's smuggling ring often meets here.

Notes On Unusual Games:

- **Grubfights**: Onlookers gamble on the attempts of a pair of young carrion caterpillar grubs (1'long) to sting each other with their paralyzing tentacles. A pastime enjoyed among both commons and nobles. A proven, thoroughbred fighting grub can fetch up to 300 gp. Goblins of the south worship these creatures and abhor the practice.
- **Sting**: A despicable amusement of the decadent classes: participants gamble on how long an attractive young victim tied naked to a table can resist the stings of a green scorpion crawling across his or her writhing body.
- **Toss**: Two players catch with a dart, knife, or axe thrown back and forth across the length of the tavern. If it hits the wall, floor, or a bystander, whoever touched it last loses.
- **Large Chess**: A bizarre and repugnant upper class indulgence. A form of half life-sized chess played on an enormous board where the role of each piece is played by a member of a species of pale, drooling, nearly braindead halfling, specifically bred for the purpose, dressed in the garb appropriate to the piece they are supposed to represent.
- **Pin the Serpent**: A player is bound to a chair with his or her hands tied and a dagger is placed (blade out) in the player's mouth. A viper is placed on the table before the player. The player attempts to stab the viper. Patrons gamble on the outcome.
- **Eye Spitting**: Contestants eat small, bioluminescent squid alive and spit their eyeballs into the snow, competing for distance.
- **Basilisk Fights**: A blind referee places two iguana-sized basilisks on a climbing frame in a closet, the door is closed, and spectators wait to hear a thudding sound. Whichever contestant's basilisk isn't in pieces on the floor wins. An extremely expensive sport. Champion basilisks bring as much as 2,000 gp.
- **Truth or Challenge**: As the child's game "truth or dare" – only the honest of the "truths" is enforced by carefully observing color changes in a hybrid orchid that eats lies.
- **Flaming Chess**: The wooden pieces are set alight before play begins, and kept that way throughout the game. Any pieces burned beyond recognition are lost.
- **Floating Sting**: As "Sting" above, only a jellyfish is used instead of a scorpion.
- **Devilswheel**: A contestant spins a wheel with the names of various common objects (purse, shoe, knife, etc.) on it, takes 3 shots, leaves the bar, and comes back with the object in 10 minutes. A witness attends to make sure the object was stolen from a stranger.

Late Edition Conversions

If you are using the version of the game that was official as of this printing, use the table below. The HD in the original monster description = Level. If you are using a different version of the game which, nevertheless, requires more information than is provided in the statblocks, assume:

- Creatures attack as ordinary fighters of a level equal to the creature's hit dice.
- 5 hit points per die or roll d8 per HD.
- Smart monsters save as typical wizards/magic-users of a level equal to their hit dice, fast or sneaky monsters save as rogues/thieves, and tough monsters as fighters/warriors.
- Initiative modifiers = +1 for most monsters, +2 for smart monsters, +3 for fast or sneaky monsters and -1 for large, armored monsters.
- Save difficulty for innate abilities is equal to 12 + creature's HD.

These guidelines should provide experienced GMs enough information to run the monsters in any version of the game. However, for GMs who are still worried, most of these monsters have analogues in official monster books that can be used to calculate missing values – if you need to know missing ability scores for the blue tiger, for instance, use the entry for "tiger", treat the flailceratops as a modified "triceratops", etc.

Immortal Zoo

Name	Init	HP/ Bloodied	AC	Fort	Ref	Will	Primary Attack	Damage	Attack	Damage	AP
Nightingale	+10	7 / 3	26	19	27	25	Command: +10 vs Will	Take an action with target			
Mutant Snail	+1	1	13	14	12	21	Slime: +0	0	You've been slimed		
Parnival, Vampire Monkey	+9	48 / 24	13	19	24	26	Bite: +17 — Can attack 4 targets	1d6+4	Grapple: +9 vs Refl	Drain 4 - ongoing Gain 4 hp per successful drain	
Xortoise	+5	122 / 61	29	30	21		Claw: +11	3d8-5			
Narcissus Peacock	+7	18 / 9	16	15	16	17	Bite: +7	1d4+3	Mesmerize: +6 vs Will (Blaze) Reloads 4-6 Stun – ongoing		
Unsettling Toad	+8	32 / 16	18	15	18	15	Bite: +5	1d4+3	Blind: +8 vs Fort (ranged) Free Action	Blind 2 days	
Mottled Fungi	+3	38 / 19	18	19	15	18	Slam: +7	1d4+3+poison			
Blue Tiger	+9	58 / 29	20	20	22	19	2xClaw: +11 follow-up	1d6+4	Bite: +9	2d8	
Firefly Woman	+2	18 / 9	14	13	15	14	Melee: +6	1d6+2	Ranged: +3	1d6+2	
White Octopus	+5	72 / 36	23	23	24		6x Tentacle: +14	1d8+5	Bite: +10 (if target grappled)	2d6+5	
Raxia & Danica	+1	12 / 6	13	13	13		Melee: +6	1d6+2			
Ozwyick, the Griffon	+6	56 / 28	21	21	22		Claw: +12	1d8+4			
Miniphant	+1	12 / 6	13	14	12	13	Gore: +4	1d4+3			
Goatscorpion	+7	64 / 32	24	22	24	21	2x Pincers: +13 vs Ref	1d8+4 grabbed save ends	Sting: +11 vs Fort	1d6 poison	
Candelabraxian	+7	72 / 36	25	25	24	24	Claw: +16	2d6+5	Gore: +14 vs Ref	8 ongoing fire	
Peryton	+8	72 / 36	24	20	23	22	2x Claw: +14	3d4+5	Sonic: Auto hit (blast) Reloads on 3-6	Hallucination d4 rounds	
Fly Demon	+8	204 / 102	29	30	27	27	Constrict: +18 vs Reflex	*/ongoing	Gaze: +16 vs Will	Stun save ends; Petrified if 2 saves failed in a row	1
Thrace, the Nagasusa, Vorkutia, the Nephildian	+8	112 / 56	23	21	24	21	Claw: +12	1d8+4	Grapple: +10 vs Ref	10 hp drain + daze ongoing	1
Gudge	+1	1	15	15	15	15	Claw: +5	4			
Flailceratops	+4	172 / 86	28	29	22	24	Slam: +19	2d6+7	Flail: +17	3d12+9	

House of the Medusa

Name	Init	HP/ Bloodied	AC	Fort	Ref	Will	Primary Attack	Damage	Attack	Damage	AP
Eshrgel the Medusa	+3	54 / 27	17	17	16	18	Touch: +8	1d8+4 acid	Gaze: +12 vs Will	Stun save ends; Petrified if 2 saves failed in a row	
Plasmic Ghoul	+5	128 / 64	24	22	24	26	Dagger: +13	1d4+4			

Library of Zorlac

Name	Init	HP/ Bloodied	AC	Fort	Ref	Will	Primary Attack	Damage	Attack	Damage	AP
Zorlac	+7	80 / 40	24	24	24	25	Dagger: +15	1d4+5	Spell: +13 vs Def	Effects up to 10th level spells	
Dividing Demon	+7	186 / 93	28	29	25	26	Claws: +17	1d8-5	Grapple: +14 vs Fort		1
Hydra Body	+5	172 / 88 +17/head	23	24	23	22	# of heads x Bite: +11	1d8+4			
Hydra Tenders	+6	44 / 22	19	18	19	20	Dagger: +9	1d4-4	Spell: +9 vs Def	Effects up to 5th level spells	
Librarians	+10	56 / 28	22	21	23	24	Melee: +13	1d6+6	Ranged: +14		
Moon	+9	26 / 13	17	18	18	17	Touch: +8	2d6+4			
Vortullax	+6	96 / 48	22	21	21	20	Ranged Bite: +15	*		1d8+4 – 1 attack gains; Ongoing 5 poison (save ends)	

This table is only intended to cover the differences between the Type 4 versions and earlier versions of the monsters given here, it is recommended that GMs running Type 4 games should still review the original monster descriptions for any details that transcend edition.

Apothecary	Armorer/Blacksmith	Art Dealer	Asylum	Baker	Bookbinder
Barber	Bowyer	Brewery	Brothel		Candlemaker
Butcher		Cheesemaker	Clockmaker	Courthouse	Glassworks
Curiosity Shop		Fortuneteller	Furrier		General Outfitter
Gambling Hall	Granary	Hatter		Jeweler	Locksmith
Lawyer	Leatherworks	Livestock Dealer/Breeder	Market hall	Mill	Nest of Criminals
Moneylender	Tavern/Inn			Ostler	
Mason		Physician	Printer/Engraver		Scholar
Private Residence	Shoemaker	Stonecarver		Tailor	Taxidermist
Theater	Veterinarian	Watchtower	Weapon-smith	Weaver	Winery	Orphanage